Jazz Session Trainer

The Woodshedder's Practice Kit
B♭ Edition

By Larry Dunlap

To access audio visit:
www.halleonard.com/mylibrary
Enter Code
2648-4876-6249-8158

ISBN 978-1-4950-2738-3

HAL•LEONARD® CORPORATION

7777 W. BLUEMOUND RD. P.O. BOX 13819 MILWAUKEE, WI 53213

In Australia Contact:
Hal Leonard Australia Pty. Ltd.
4 Lentara Court
Cheltenham, Victoria, 3192 Australia
Email: ausadmin@halleonard.com.au

Copyright © 2015 by HAL LEONARD CORPORATION
International Copyright Secured   All Rights Reserved

No part of this publication may be reproduced in any form or by
any means without the prior written permission of the Publisher.

Visit Hal Leonard Online at
www.halleonard.com

ABOUT THE AUTHOR

Larry Dunlap is a respected arranger, composer, pianist, and teacher living in the San Francisco Bay area. His playing and writing have been heard in performance and/or on numerous recordings with Bobbe Norris (his wife), Dame Cleo Laine, Mark Murphy, Sheila Jordan, violinist Jeremy Cohen, and others.

Larry has taught piano and orchestration privately and at the Stanford Jazz Workshop and Mills College. He has been the recipient of a grant from the National Endowment for the Arts and has been commissioned to write several pieces. His compositions and orchestrations have been performed by big bands, orchestras, string quartets, chamber groups, and opera companies.

He has been chief music editor for Sher Music Company for over 15 years and recently completed two books for Hal Leonard Corporation, *The Real Jazz Solos Book* and *The II–V–I Progression*. He has been particularly associated with Cape Verdean composer Amandio Cabral on over ten recordings.

At home in many styles of music, he maintains a busy career writing and playing throughout the U.S., Europe, and Japan.

CONTENTS

Introduction 4

Chapter 1   Jam Session Etiquette 5

Chapter 2   Use of Scales in Improvising 7

Chapter 3   Exercises to Improve Chops 10

Chapter 4   Jazz Etudes 19

Chapter 5   Licks – Short Phrases Inspired by Jazz Greats 32

Chapter 6   Introductions and Endings 52

Chapter 7   Practice Suggestions and a Practice Planner 61

Chapter 8   50 Frequently Played Tunes –
            Chord Charts and Online Audio 64

INTRODUCTION

Taking part in a jam session – or "jazz session," as it is presented here – is one of the most valuable and rewarding activities any developing (or well-developed) jazz musician can engage in. This is where he or she interacts with other musicians in the spontaneous creation of solos and approaches to the more commonly performed jazz tunes, from classic jazz compositions to show tunes to any other tunes known by the participating players.

In the first part of this book, you will find basic information about the etiquette of these music sessions and what you need to know to participate in them. These are useful guidelines for instrumentalists and vocalists alike.

Following this, we provide some tools that will help you become a more proficient improviser. Chords and scales are the building blocks of spontaneous jazz creation. The scales presented are just a starting point in what every musician needs to know about these basics. Next are exercises, etudes, and "licks" to develop phrasing and melodic understanding. Here you will find concepts that will – we hope – inspire you to create your own musical ideas.

The material on Introductions and Endings presents many suggestions for beginning and ending tunes in a jam session setting. Most of these examples are commonly known among more experienced jazz musicians, but they have rarely been presented in written texts. Some musicians, I'm sure, will find this the most valuable chapter in this book. After this, a few thoughts about a practice routine are presented.

And finally, you will find a list of tunes that are commonly played in jazz (or jam) sessions. Fifty of these compositions are included on the accompanying online audio as play-along tunes with corresponding chord charts. While the melodies are not included, the written charts follow the forms of the tunes on the audio and are an important resource for practicing soloing and becoming familiar with well-known chord progressions.

I hope you will find a wealth of material in these pages to prepare you to join in on spontaneous musical adventures with other jazz musicians. Jam sessions, or "jazz sessions," are the heart and soul of this wonderfully creative path in the world of music.

"Straight ahead and strive for tone."

–Larry Dunlap

Chapter 1: Jam Session Etiquette

There are really two types of jam sessions. One type is when fully experienced musicians get together in an impromptu setting to play on commonly known tunes in a less structured way than they would in a concert situation. They have a freedom they normally would not have in a more formal setting, although these jam sessions have sometimes been organized for concert performances with a paying (or not paying) audience. Many of the high points in jazz have been achieved in these situations. These are often called "cutting sessions" and can become quite heated and competitive.

The more common jam session is when players of various levels of experience get together to play commonly known tunes with little structure other than the tune itself and perhaps a commonly known intro or ending. These can be completely without organization or, more often, with a rhythm section or core group of players providing the foundation for musicians sitting in.

These jam sessions with accomplished and less experienced musicians playing together are an important part of a musician's development in playing jazz. They are an opportunity for a developing musician to get comfortable with tunes they are learning and to try out ideas and improvisations without the pressures of "performing" in front of a discerning audience that probably has paid some money to hear an organized concert.

It is a chance for blossoming players to play and learn alongside more skilled musicians, an ideal place to get some practical experience. Criticism is not often given. More frequently, a young player will find encouragement and support, even if their efforts are not up to the level of some of the people with whom they are playing.

A developing musician should actively seek out situations where they can take part in a jam session or even just observe. It is generally an exciting event that leads to experimentation and innovation. To be a part of a jam session is to be a part of the essence of jazz.

That being said, there are some guidelines to be aware of when a young player wants to jump into this heady environment and join in the fun and improvisation that are the heart and soul of experience. Some of these are "rules" for jam sessions in general; others are things that a less experienced player needs to consider when he wants to play.

- There should be an accomplished musician who leads the jam session. This person would oversee the inviting of other musicians to take part. While a musician sitting in would often call the tune and count off the tempo, in many circumstances the leader might count off the tune so it is not uncomfortably fast or slow for everyone to play. This is particularly true if the rhythm section is playing non-stop.

- A sign-up sheet is a good idea, particularly if there are many musicians who want to play. The leader would call the musicians up to play. More often than not, the more accomplished players play the first solos, with the less adept following with their own solos. In a way, this seems backward. Try to vary this type of order of solos. If there is a sign-up sheet, players are generally invited to play in the order they have signed up.

- Be sure you know what you are playing. Do not call a tune or play on a tune if you do not know it. You should know the melody and chords, but you could play a solo on the chord progression if you don't know the melody. Just don't join in on the melody. When it is your turn to call a tune, call something you know well and are comfortable with.

- If there is a tune you want to play that is not in the mainstream jazz repertoire, you might be able to present it if you bring charts for everyone. Don't be afraid to do that, but go with the leader's wishes if he or she doesn't want to try the tune.

- Show respect for the other musicians, particularly the more experienced ones. If you get a chance, ask them for suggestions on how to improve your playing.

- Limit the number of choruses you play. Three or four choruses is a good length for a fast or medium tempo tune. One chorus on a ballad is usually sufficient. Playing too many choruses will quickly make you an unpopular member of the band. You might be asked to leave the stage or not be asked to play again.

- If you find that you are not as prepared as you should be to take part in a jam session with higher level players, go home and spend some constructive time learning tunes and working on your improvisational skills.

- As in any music situation, listen to the other musicians, particularly the rhythm section. Get clues from the bass, drums and piano as to what rhythmic or harmonic variations they might be introducing into the music. Don't hesitate to take things in your own direction or to go with them in theirs. At the same time, do not impose your musical will on everyone else if they are not going with you.

- Rhythm Section Players: You are greatly valued in a jam session. If there are many players for your instrument, you need to be patient and wait to be called up. Like horn players or vocalists, you might be able to play only one tune. On the other hand, if there are no other players for your instrument, you may be playing constantly, a sometimes quite tiring experience.

- It is an unnecessary cliché to have horn solos first, followed by rhythm section solos (piano, then bass, then drums). Vary this, so that sometimes rhythm section solos are first.

- A good jam session has a lot of variety in tempos, styles, and repertoire. If you are asked to choose a tune and a ballad has just been played, it is probably not a good idea to call another ballad.

- Singers: Be sure you know the song you want to sing as well as the key and tempo you would like. Be prepared. Either have charts for everyone or be able to describe in detail what you want in the way of introduction, form, and ending. Sing what you sing well. If you are not a jazz singer, whatever that is, sing in a style with which you're conversant. The good musicians will follow you. If there are a number of singers, do not automatically expect to sing more than one song. If you are exceptionally good, you may be asked to sing another.

- Above all, have a fun and creative time. Remember to be respectful of the other musicians and leave your ego at home.

In the following pages, you will find materials that will help prepare you for joining in jam sessions. We will examine useful scales, present a sampling of exercises to improve your facility, explore some etudes written to the chord changes of common jam session tunes, meet many choice licks to play over small harmonic cells, and find chord charts to 50 commonly played jam session tunes.

There is a lot of information included here. With diligent practice, you should become more comfortable in your playing with other musicians and have many years to continue your development in this amazing art form, jazz.

chapter 2
Use of Scales in Improvising

When an experienced jazz musician sees a chord name, he or she most often thinks of the notes of the chord first, then the possible extension and alteration of the chord, and then a scale that will go with this chord. One approach to improvising, then, is to know the scales that most often go with certain chords and to choose notes based on those scales – with variations and additions, of course.

The scales below are a good place to start. They are presented in the key of C for ease of reading, but should be learned in all keys. Seven of these scales are the modes; the final four are scales with more altered tones.

CHORDS

C, C6, Cmaj7, Cmaj9   Ionian (major scale)

C7. C9, C9sus, C13   Mixolydian (major scale with ♭7)

Cm, Cm6, Cm7, Cm9   Dorian (♭3, ♭7)

Cm, Cm7   Aeolian (♭3, ♭6)

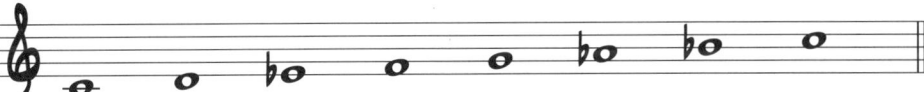

Cm♭9(♭13)   Phrygian (♭2, ♭6, ♭7)

Cm7♭5   Locrian (♭2, ♭3, ♭5, ♭6, ♭7)

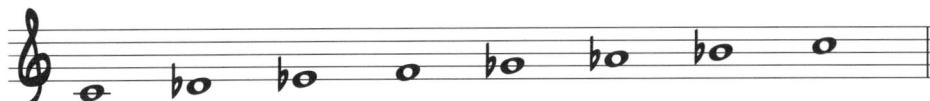

Cmaj7♭5, Cmaj7, Cmaj9   Lydian (major with ♯4)

C7, C7♭5, C9, C9♭5,   Lydian ♭7 (major with ♯4, ♭7)
C13, C13♯11

C7♯5, C7♭5, C7♯5(♭9),   Diminished Whole Tone (♯2, ♯4, ♯5, ♭7, ♭9)
C7♯5(♯9)

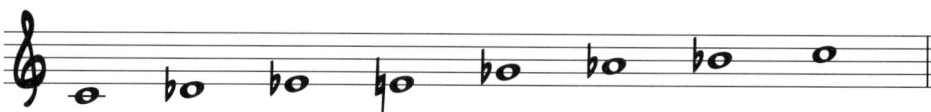

Cø7, Cm♭5(maj7)   Symmetrical Diminished (whole/half)

C7♭5(♯9), C7♭5(♭9),   Symmetrical Diminished (half/whole)
C13♯5(♯9), C7♯5(♭9)

There follow a few other scales that are useful.

Used over a single chord (C7 or Cm7) or a series of chords in a C tonality when you want a "bluesy" feel. Sometimes used for entire Blues choruses. Best if used with discretion.   Blues Scale

C6, Cmaj7, C6/9, C7, C9   Major Pentatonic

Cm6, Cm7, Cm6/9,   Minor Pentatonic
Cm9

8

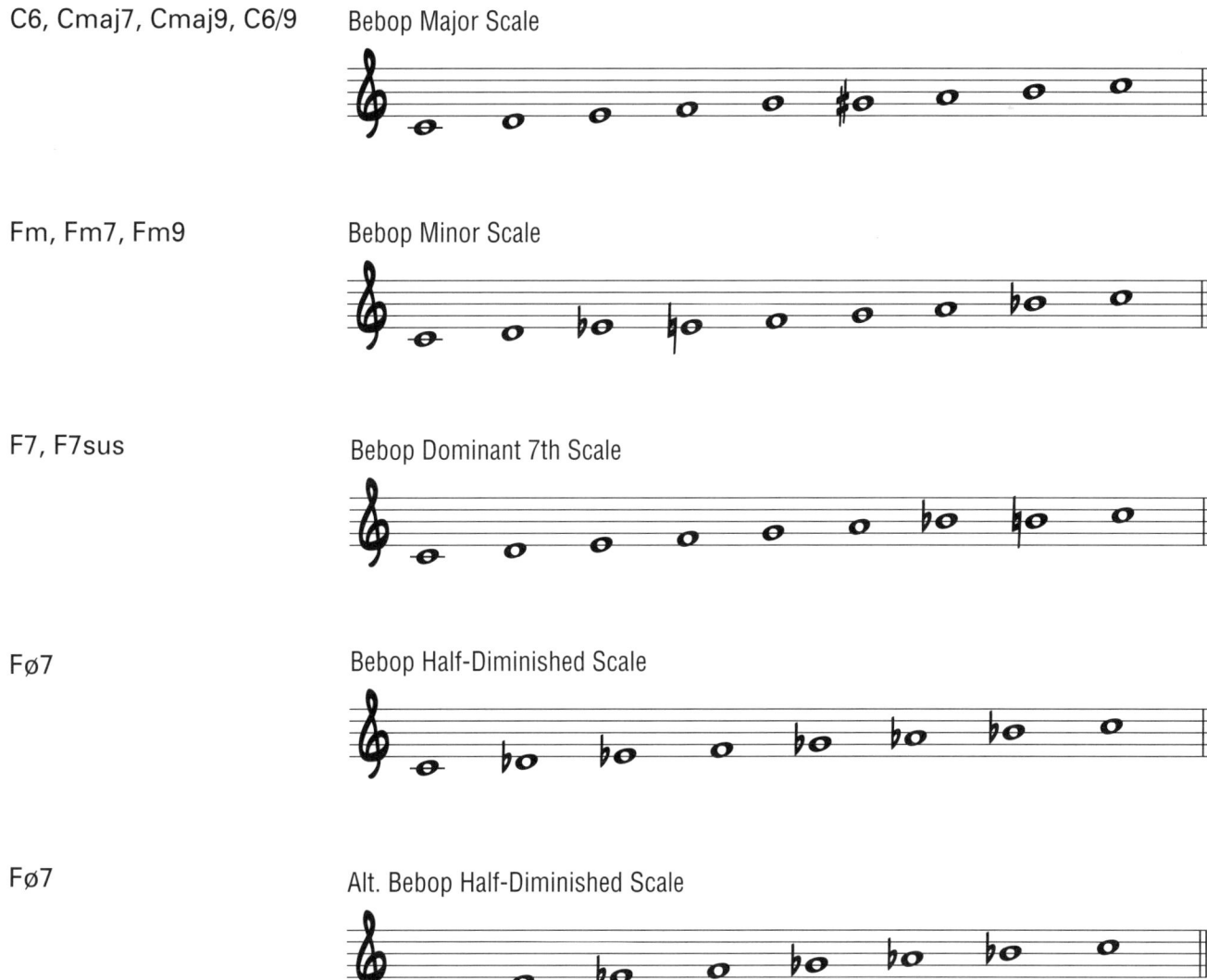

The Dorian scale or the Aeolian scale may be appropriate to use over a minor 7th chord. Determine whether the melody or soloist includes a major 6th (Dorian) or a minor 6th (Aeolian).

To become familiar and comfortable with scales, do more than just practice the scale as written. Play the scale notes in random order and in varying rhythms. Recognize the sound of each chord and scale. Be sure to work with the scales in all keys.

There are additional scales not listed here, so do some further study. A great book is Steve Barta's *The Source* (published by Hal Leonard, HL00240885); it's perfect for musicians, teachers, or anyone looking for solid info on scales and chords, and how they work together. Develop your own scales and approaches to create a unique sound.

chapter 3
Exercises to Improve Chops

The following exercises are written for all levels of players and are just a few examples of the types of material you will find in exercise books for jazz musicians. The exercises range in length from one to four measures. Each is played either over one chord or over a short chord progression. Transpose portions of an exercise up or down an octave as needed. It also is extremely important that exercises such as these be played in all keys so that you become comfortable in all tonal centers.

Exercise 1

Exercise 2

Exercise 3

Exercise 4

Exercise 5

Exercise 6

C♯7♭9
D7♭9
E♭7♭9
E7♭9
F7♭9
F♯7♭9

Exercise 7

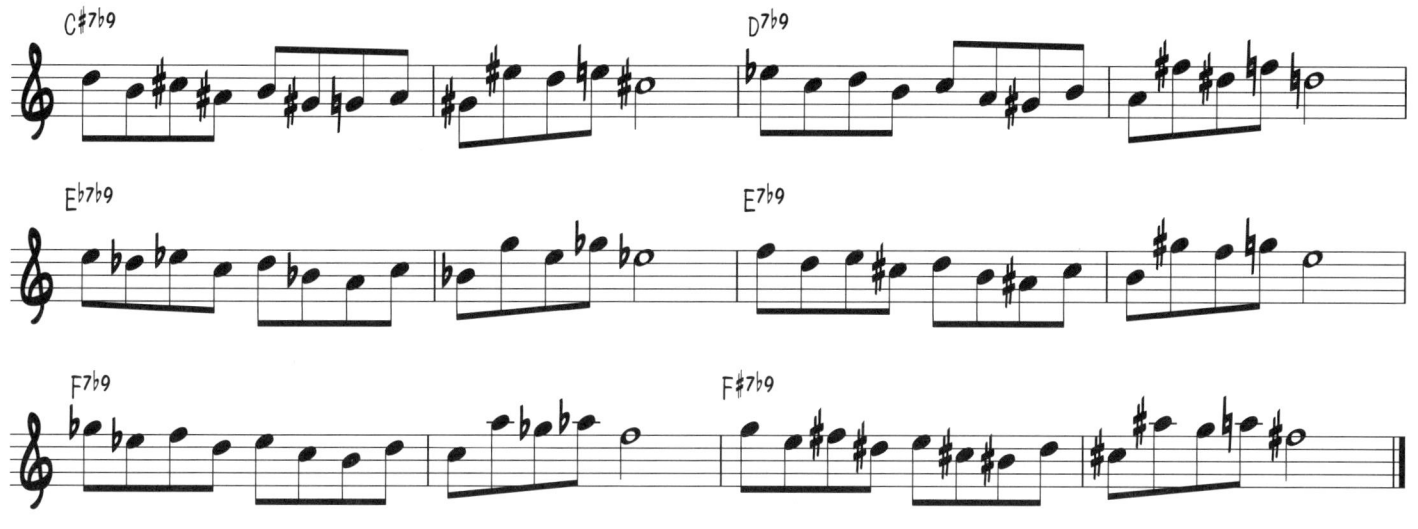

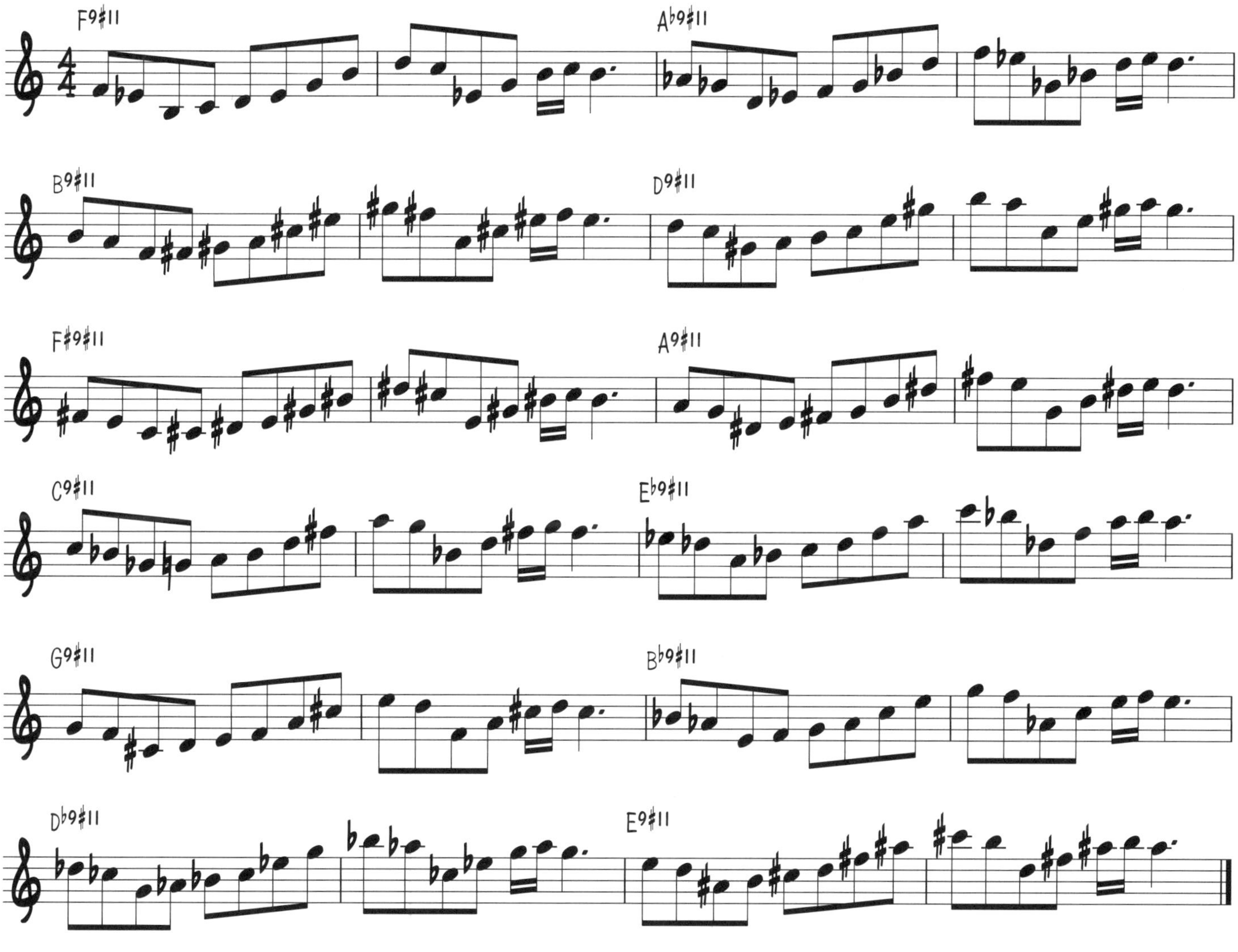
F9♯11
A♭9♯11
B9♯11
D9♯11
F♯9♯11
A9♯11
C9♯11
E♭9♯11
G9♯11
B♭9♯11
D♭9♯11
E9♯11

Exercise 8

Exercise 9

Em7♭5 A7♭9 Dm7 E♭m7♭5 A♭7♭9 D♭m7
Dm7♭5 G7♭9 Cm7 C♯m7♭5 F♯7♭9 Bm7
Cm7♭5 F7♭9 B♭m7 Bm7♭5 E7♭9 Am7

Exercise 10

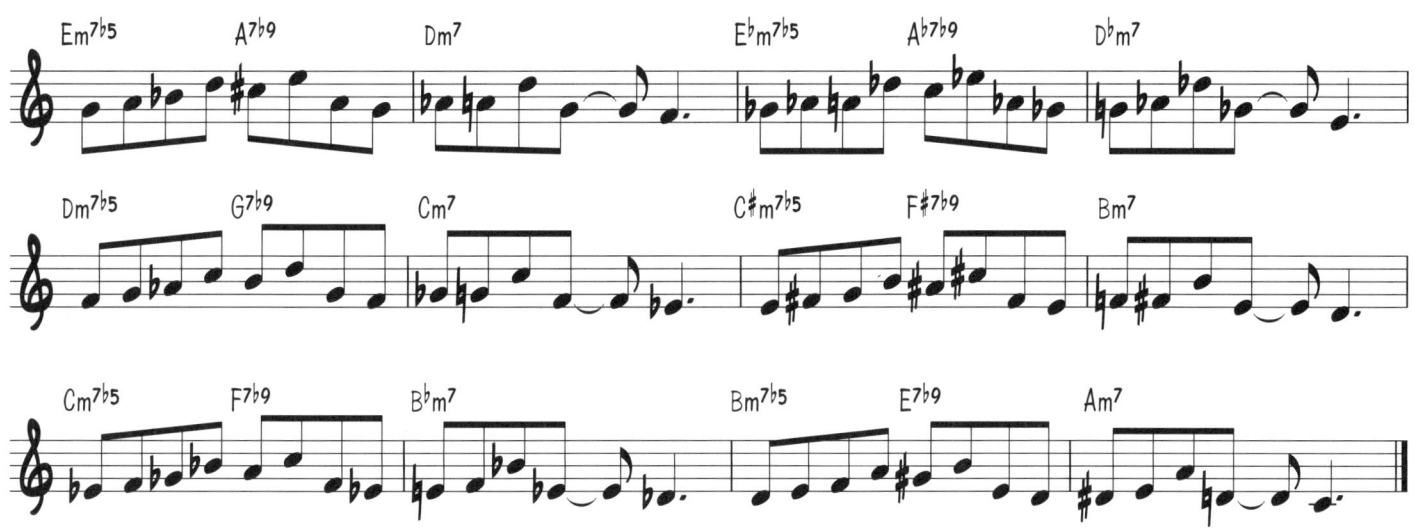

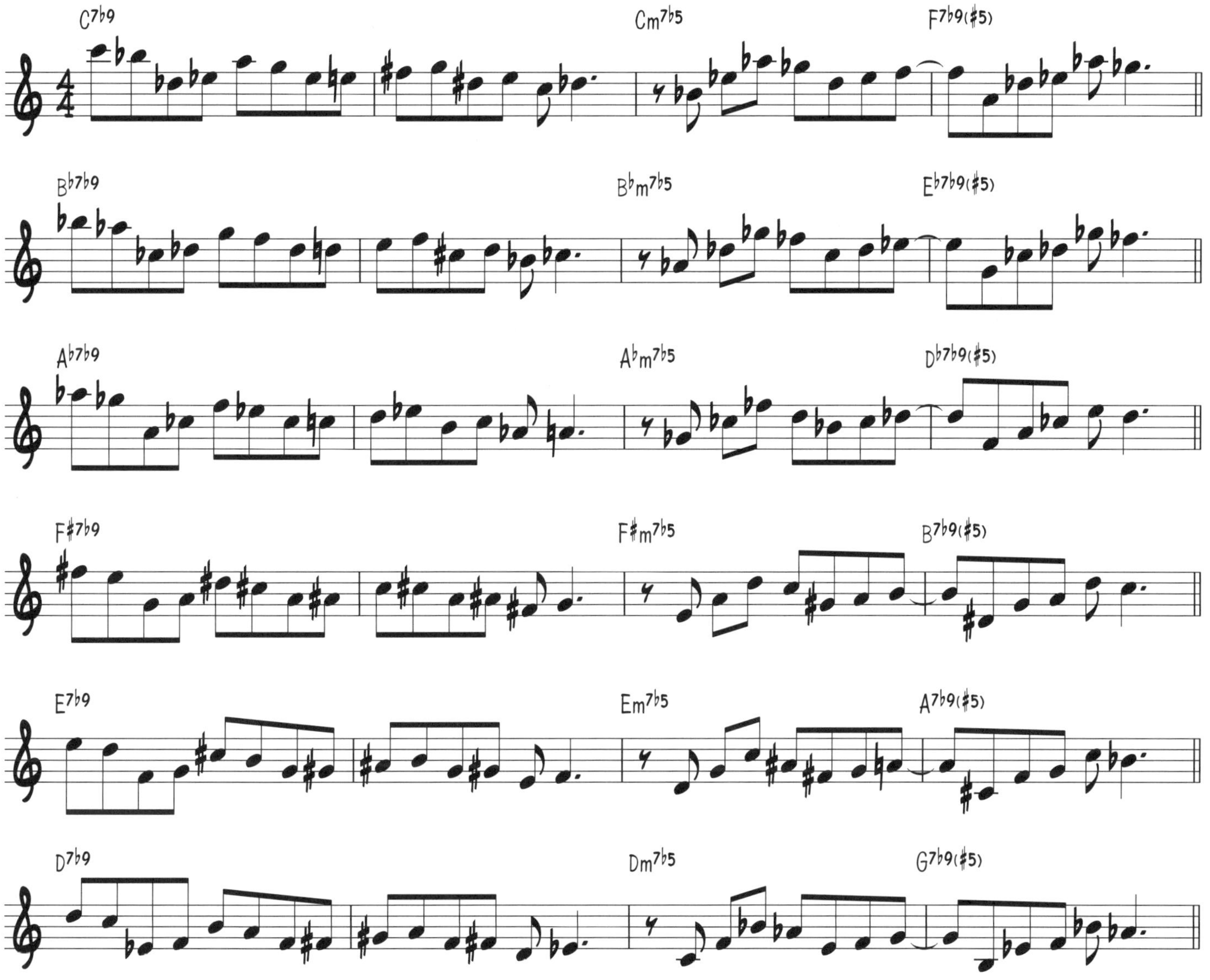
C7♭9 Cm7♭5 F7♭9(♯5)
B♭7♭9 B♭m7♭5 E♭7♭9(♯5)
A♭7♭9 A♭m7♭5 D♭7♭9(♯5)
F♯7♭9 F♯m7♭5 B7♭9(♯5)
E7♭9 Em7♭5 A7♭9(♯5)
D7♭9 Dm7♭5 G7♭9(♯5)

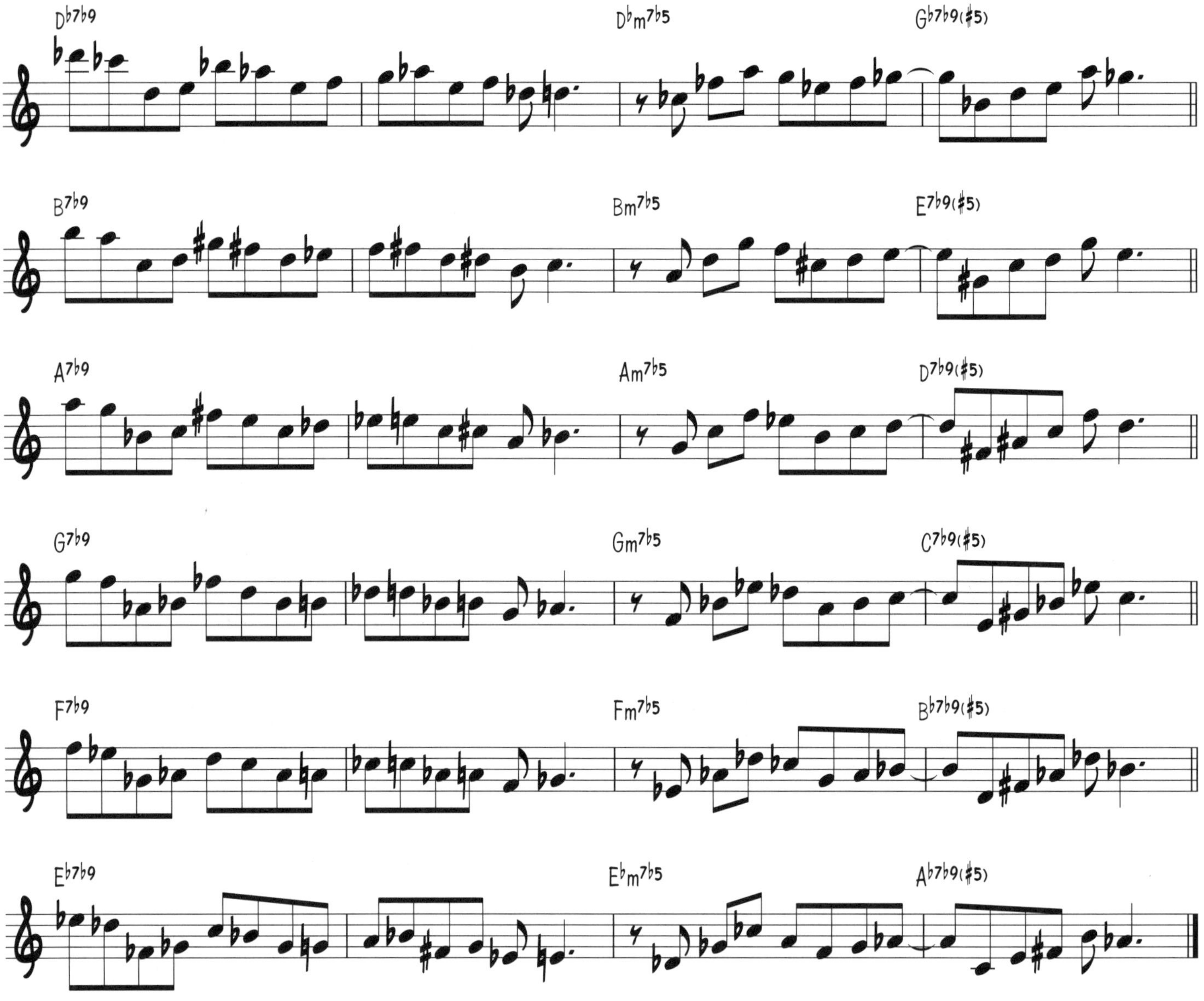
D♭7♭9
D♭m7♭5
G♭7♭9(♯5)
B7♭9
Bm7♭5
E7♭9(♯5)
A7♭9
Am7♭5
D7♭9(♯5)
G7♭9
Gm7♭5
C7♭9(♯5)
F7♭9
Fm7♭5
B♭7♭9(♯5)
E♭7♭9
E♭m7♭5
A♭7♭9(♯5)

Exercise 11

Cm7
F7♭9
B♭maj7
G7♭9
Cm7
F7
B♭maj7
C♯m7
F♯7♭9
Bmaj7
G♯7♭9
C♯m7
F♯7
Bmaj7
Dm7
G7♭9
Cmaj7
A7♭9
Dm7
G7
Cmaj7

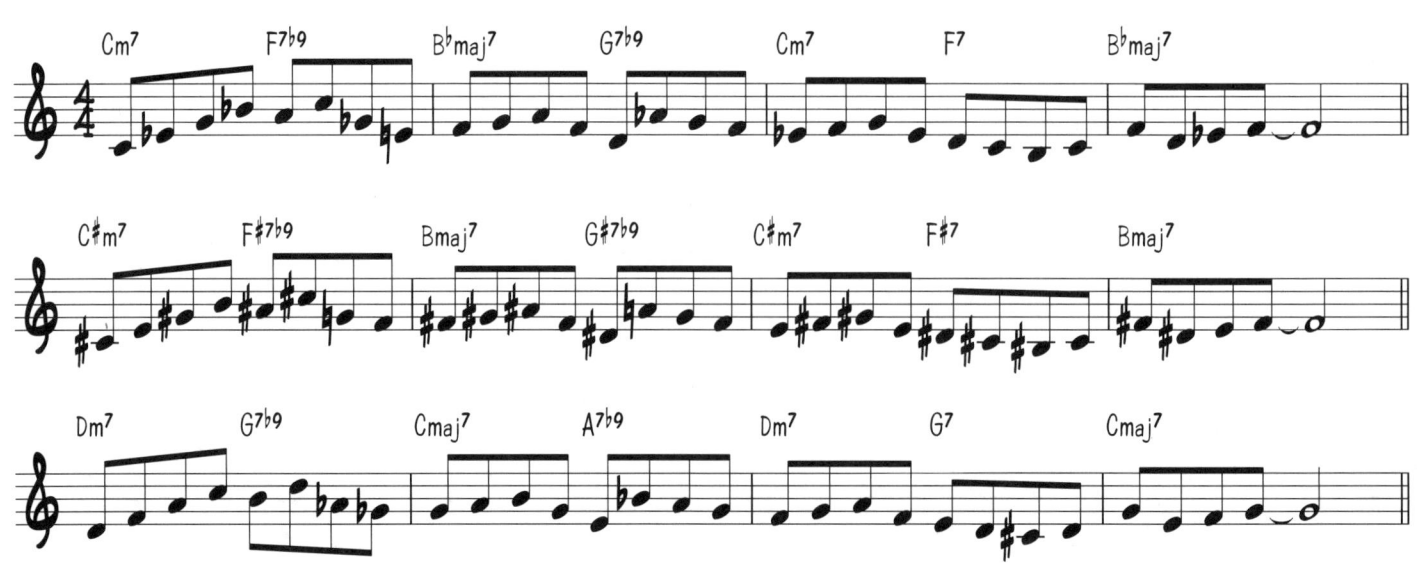

You've probably discovered that there are many books of exercises to improve your technique and strength on an instrument. Below is a list of exercise books that you may find useful. We should point out, though, that this is just a brief sampling of what is available. Do some exploring to find the ones that appeal to you and that are appropriate for your level of playing and experience.

The Cycle of Fifths by Emile DeCosmo and Laura De Cosmo (Hal Leonard Corporation, 00311114)
> This book provides more than 450 exercises, including hundreds of melodic and rhythmic ideas. The book is designed to help improvisers master the cycle of fifths, one of the primary progressions in music.

Exercises and Etudes for the Jazz Instrumentalist by J. J. Johnson
Treble Clef Edition (Hal Leonard Corporation, HL 00842042)
Bass Clef Edition (Hal Leonard Corporation, HL 00842018)
> A collection of original pieces designed as study material and playable by any instrument, these pieces (the harmonies of which are based on well-known standards) run the gamut of the jazz experience, featuring common and uncommon time signatures and keys, and styles from ballads to funk. They are progressively graded so that both beginners and professionals will be challenged by the demands of this wonderful music.

Line Games: An In-Depth Study of Single-Note Lines for Guitar by Randy Vincent (Sher Music Co.)
> Though aimed at guitar players, the material in this book is extremely valuable for any instrumentalist.

The Serious Jazz Practice Book for All Instruments: Melodic Materials for the Modern Jazz Soloist by Barry Finnerty (Sher Music Co.)
> This useful publication takes all the diatonic, pentatonic, chromatic, whole-tone and diminished scales and gives you step-by-step exercises that dissect them into hundreds of useable patterns.

Tons of Runs for the Contemporary Pianist by Andy LaVerne (Ekay Music, Inc.)
> Here's a wide-ranging compendium of runs, licks, and lines found in the jazz vernacular, each written in three different keys, and presented in a straightforward style

21 Bebop Exercises by Steve Rawlins (Hal Leonard Corporation, HL00315341)
> This book/CD pack is both a warm-up collection and a manual for bebop phrasing. Its tasty and sophisticated exercises are designed for both vocalists and instrumentalists interested in further developing their proficiency with jazz interpretation.

Velocity Exercises and Etudes for the Jazz Musician by Jordon Ruwe (Houston Publishing, Inc., distributed by Hal Leonard Corporation, HL00030456)
> This helpful study guide for all treble clef instruments includes 25 exercises to help players increase their speed, plus seven etudes based on famous jazz chord progressions.

Books by Greg Fishman also are worth exploring.
> Check out his website at gregfishmanjazzstudios.com.

Chapter 4: Jazz Etudes

The following 12 jazz etudes are, first and foremost, an attempt to familiarize the player with the expressive aspects of jazz, whether it be a swing style, ballad playing, Latin style, or even-eighth-note style. They are written over the chord changes to common jazz tunes that you might encounter at a jam session. Though akin to written-out solo choruses, they are not meant to be memorized and performed as solos.

In an effort to have these etudes accessible to musicians who are just starting to join in jazz sessions, they are written at an intermediate (or, in some instances, lower intermediate) level. At the same time, advanced players will enjoy sight reading through them and will, we hope, find some challenges.

Most of the etudes are considered medium swing – with a bossa nova, a ballad, and an up-tempo swing thrown in for good measure. However, the charts can be approached and played in various tempos. You might want to start slowly and increase the tempo of some exercises so they remain challenging. Feel free to create your own phrasing and articulations.

Etude 1

Etude 2

Etude 3

Etude 4

Medium Swing

23

Etude 5

Medium Swing

Etude 6

Bossa Nova

Etude 7

Etude 8

Medium Swing

Etude 9

Up-tempo Swing

Etude 10

Etude 11

Etude 12

Ballad

There are, of course, many books of etudes available, both in the jazz idiom and in other styles. In addition to the books by J.J. Johnson and Jordan Ruwe referenced on page 18, take a look at the following publication:

Stylistic Etudes in the Jazz Idiom, compiled by Lou Fisher (Houston Publishing, Inc., distributed by Hal Leonard Corporation, HL00841045)
    120 etudes composed by seven respected jazz performers/educators. Contains five etudes each in swing, ballad, and Latin/funk categories, beginning at a medium level and progressing in difficulty. Includes a total of 15 etudes each for saxophones, trumpet, trombone, bass trombone, piano, guitar, bass and drums.

Chapter 5: Licks – Short Phrases Inspired by Jazz Greats

On the following pages you will find a variety of short phrases (or "licks") that have been inspired by solos from many of the greatest performers in jazz. They are played over a single chord or a short chord progression and are just a few examples of what might be played in these harmonic situations.

Think of licks as melodic sentences that have been practiced and absorbed by individual players, to be inserted into a solo when a certain chord or chord sequence is encountered. They could be this or they could be completely spontaneous. Usually a listener would not know, unless a lick is repeated several times.

The licks in this chapter are mostly intermediate level lines. There are no stylistic or tempo designations. While just about all of them will sound good played with a swing feel, most of them would also work in an even-eighth-note situation in Latin or funk music. Try them with different tempos and feels.

These etudes stick mainly to the chord notes and scales of the chords. Nothing too adventurous or "outside" is here. You can find many books of licks and transcribed solos that will introduce you to more advanced improvisational ideas. For a wealth of solo transcriptions in all styles, I recommend *The Real Jazz Solos Book* by this author, Larry Dunlap (published by Hal Leonard Corporation, HL00240268).

As with all jazz exercises, it is vital that they be played in many different keys. Think about the intervals and the notes of the chord or scale and transpose them. This will increase your musical vocabulary, and will give you great practice in transposing.

These licks are presented under various groupings (Single Major Chord, Single Minor Chord, Single Dominant Chord, II-V-I Progression, etc.). Each category begins with simpler phrases and continues with somewhat more advanced ideas.

Phrases over the II-V-I Progression (major and minor) outnumber the other classifications. This three-chord sequence is the most prominent progression in jazz and popular music. For many more examples of phrases to play over II-V-I, see *The II-V-I Progression*, written by Larry Dunlap (Hal Leonard Corporation, HL00843239).

Come up with licks that will create an individual sound and style for you. Learn from the masters, certainly, but find your own path in music. The world does not need another Charlie Parker or Bill Evans, great as they were. It needs new and innovative voices that have a respect for the past, but find unique ways to express musical ideas.

Single Major Chord

Single Minor Chord

Single Dominant Chord

II-V-I Major Progression, with variations and extensions

II-V-I Minor Progression, with variations and extensions

II-VI-II-V and III-VI-II-V Major Progression, with variations and extensions

Circle of Fifths (descending), with variations and extensions

I-I7-IV-♯IVdim-I (and portions), with variations and extensions

II-V Minor, with variations and extensions

I-II-V-I Progression, with variations and extension

V-I and I-V-I Major and Minor Progressions, with variations and extensions

II-V-III-VI Progression, with variations and extensions

Other Miscellaneous Progressions

chapter 6

Introductions and Endings

In a jam session, introductions and endings are usually improvised on the spot. A few songs, however, have specific intros that are almost considered part of the tune. These include "Satin Doll," "Star Eyes," "A Night in Tunisia," and "Take the 'A' Train." Somewhat less common are specific endings for tunes. When you find a clearly stated intro or ending in a fake book, it is a good idea to learn it as a frequently played, but optional, part of the tune.

Intros and endings are usually improvised by the rhythm section, although sometimes a soloist will ad lib over an intro. A soloist will nearly always continue playing over an extended ending. A single instrument (piano, bass, drums, guitar, etc.) may improvise an intro alone. That way, there is no one else playing who might go in a different musical direction.

INTRODUCTIONS

There are many well-known short chord progressions that are used for intros. These are generally four measures long (sometimes repeated) or perhaps a two-measure vamp that is repeated indefinitely until the melody of the tune is started.

The examples in this chapter offer ideas of what might be played as an intro. For the sake of simplicity, all these intro ideas are written in C major (for tunes in a major key) or D minor (for tunes in a minor key). They should be learned in all keys. They are nothing more than chord progressions, over which the pianist or other soloist can improvise. They can also be played as chordal rhythms without a solo line.

Often the best way to set up the tune is to play the last four measures of either the full song or the bridge. Either would prepare the beginning harmonically. In a commendable effort not to "give away" the song, the melody should not be played, just the chord progression with perhaps an ad lib solo line on top. However, it might be a good idea to make use of harmonic or melodic material from the tune, maybe in an obscure way.

There are countless ways a tune can be set up. The most reasonable for a jam session is a simple harmonic idea that can be used in many situations. Often just utilizing a substitute chord or two to a familiar progression like I-VI-II-V will create enough variety to keep things interesting.

Intros when the first chord in the tune is a tonic (I) major chord
I-VI-II-V Intro

In this progression, the roots of the chords are I-VI-II-V. The note values can vary, but generally it's either two beats per chord or four beats per chord. Repeat the progression if you want, or play it as a vamp until the melody enters. Chord substitutions are always possible, particularly if everyone is listening carefully to everyone else. (Always a good idea.)

4 beats per chord

Variation

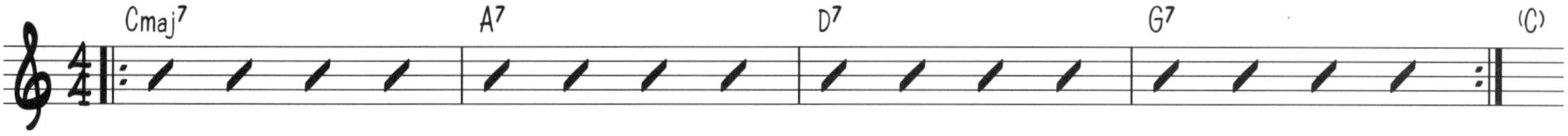

Cmaj7 A7 D7 G7 (C)

Variation

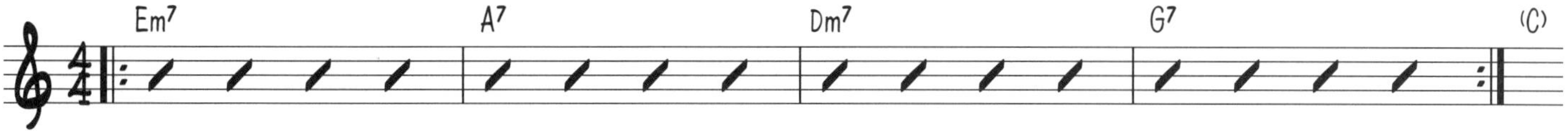

Em7 A7 Dm7 G7 (C)

Variation

Em7 E♭7 Dm7 D♭7 (C)

or 2 beats per chord

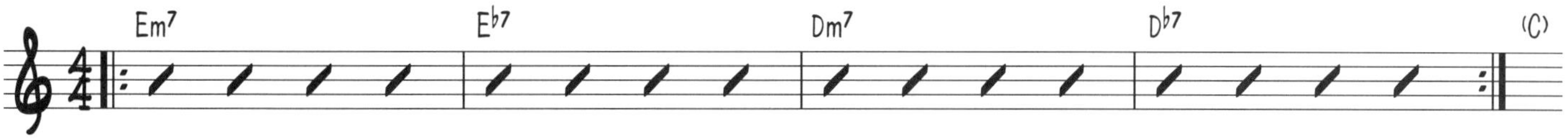

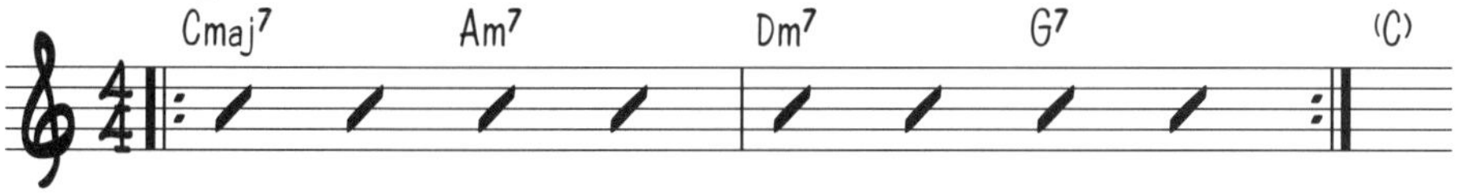

Cmaj7 Am7 Dm7 G7 (C)

Variation

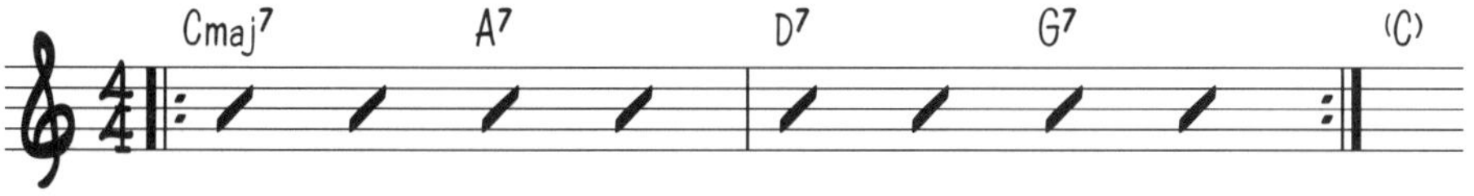

Cmaj7 A7 D7 G7 (C)

A more radical alternative

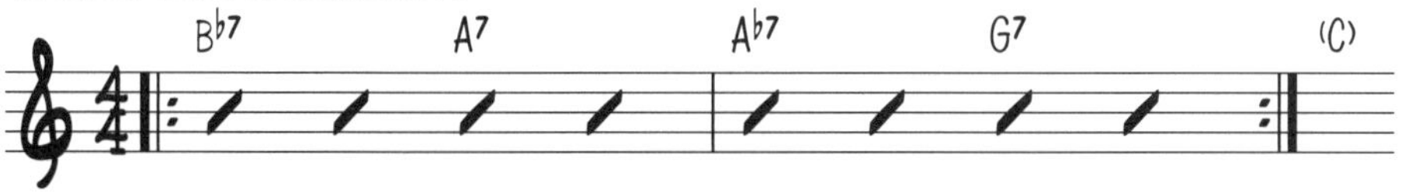

B♭7 A7 A♭7 G7 (C)

Other Possible Intros

Here are a few more ideas for introductions for tunes that begin on the tonic chord in a major key. Some of these are a bit more involved and might be more intricate than you would want to try without some planning and more communication between the musicians.

F♯m7♭5 Fm6 Em7 E♭m7 Dm7 G7 C A7 Dm7 G7 (C)

Cmaj7 F7 Em7 A7 Dm7 G7 C E♭7 Dm7 D♭7 (C)

Cmaj7 B♭7 A♭7 G7 (C)

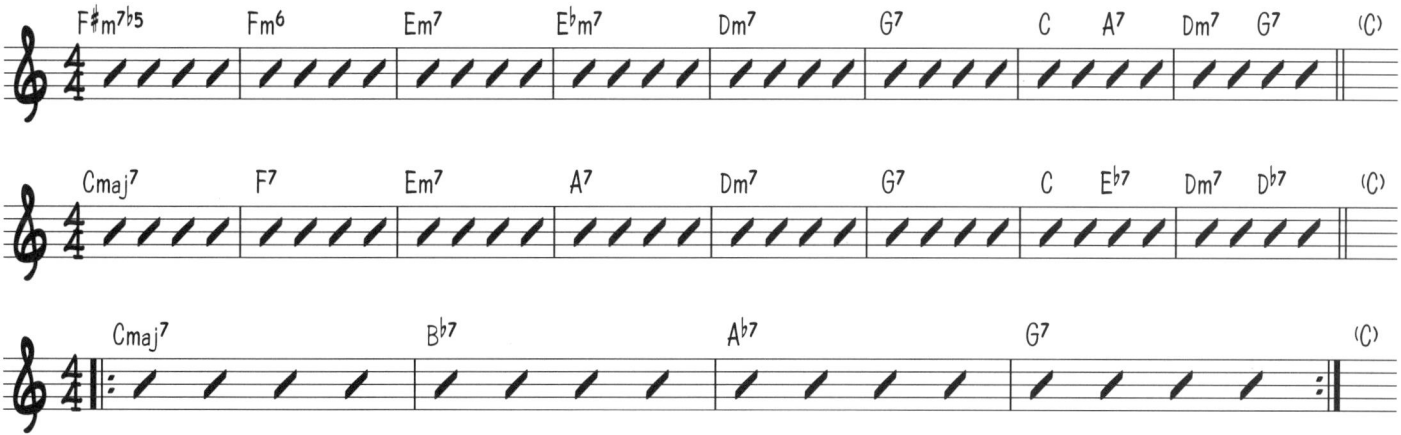

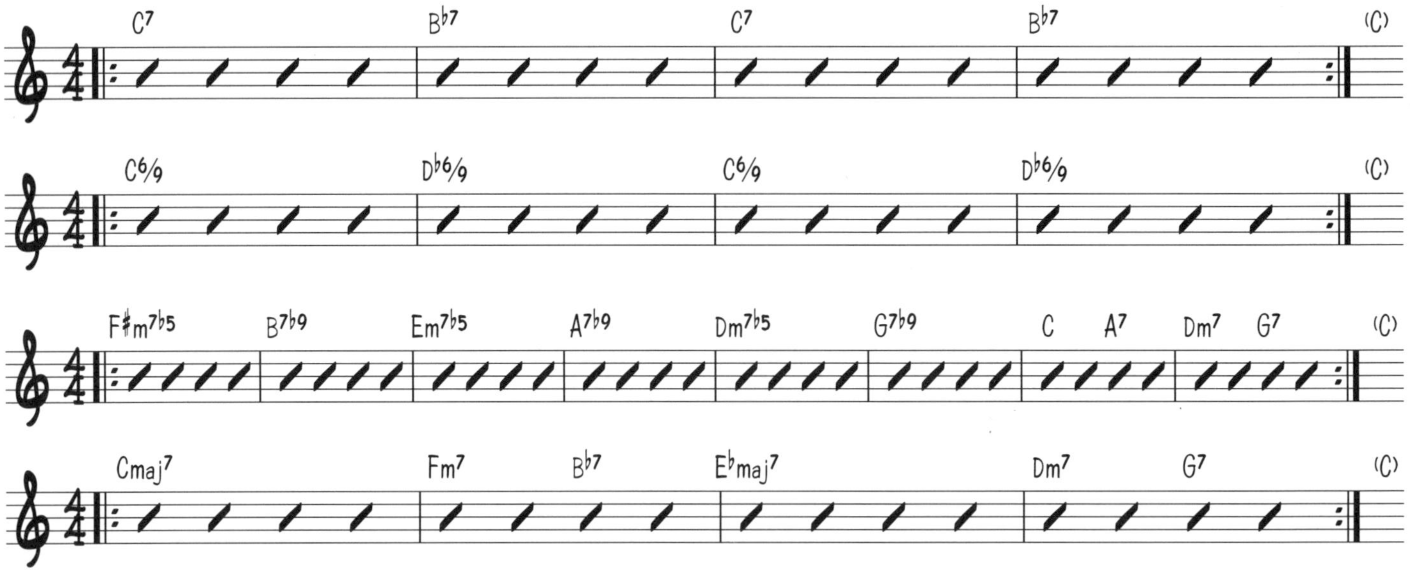

Intros over a pedal V (G in the key of C)

With a pedal fifth of the tonic key, whether major or minor, there are many possibilities for harmonies that can be played. Here are just a few examples.

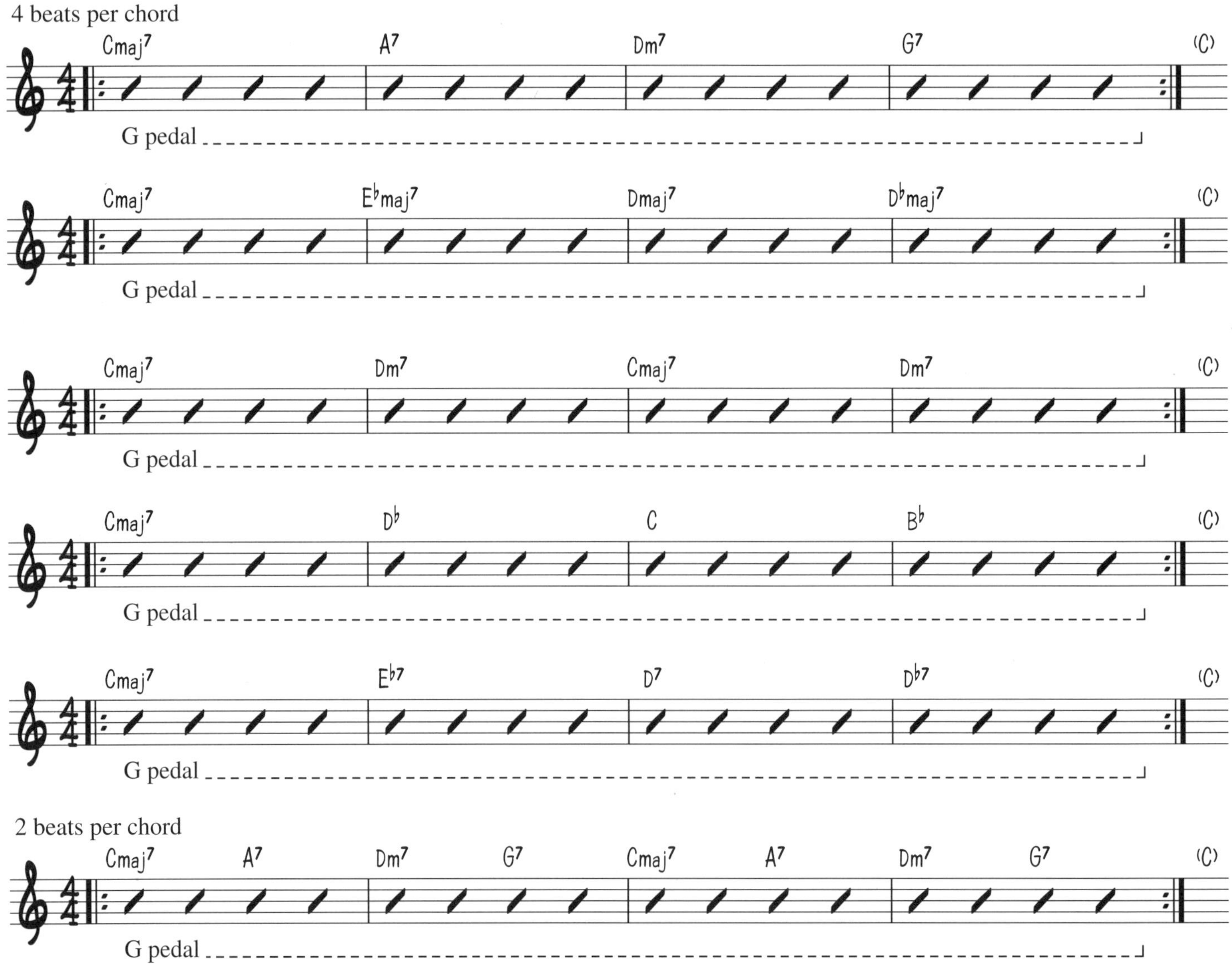

4 beats per chord

2 beats per chord

Another Simple Alternative

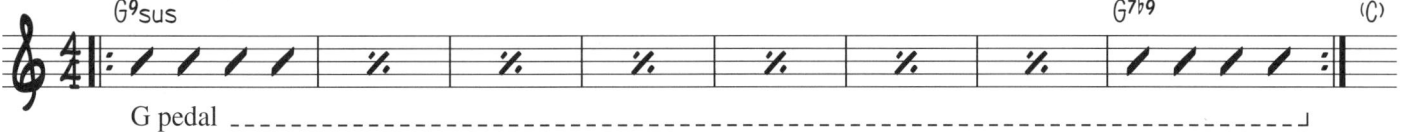

Intros when the first chord in the tune is a II minor chord

Many tunes in a major key begin on the II chord, which is a minor 7th chord. Following are a few intros you could use on this type of tune. (Often, an intro for a tune that begins on the I chord will work in this situation.)

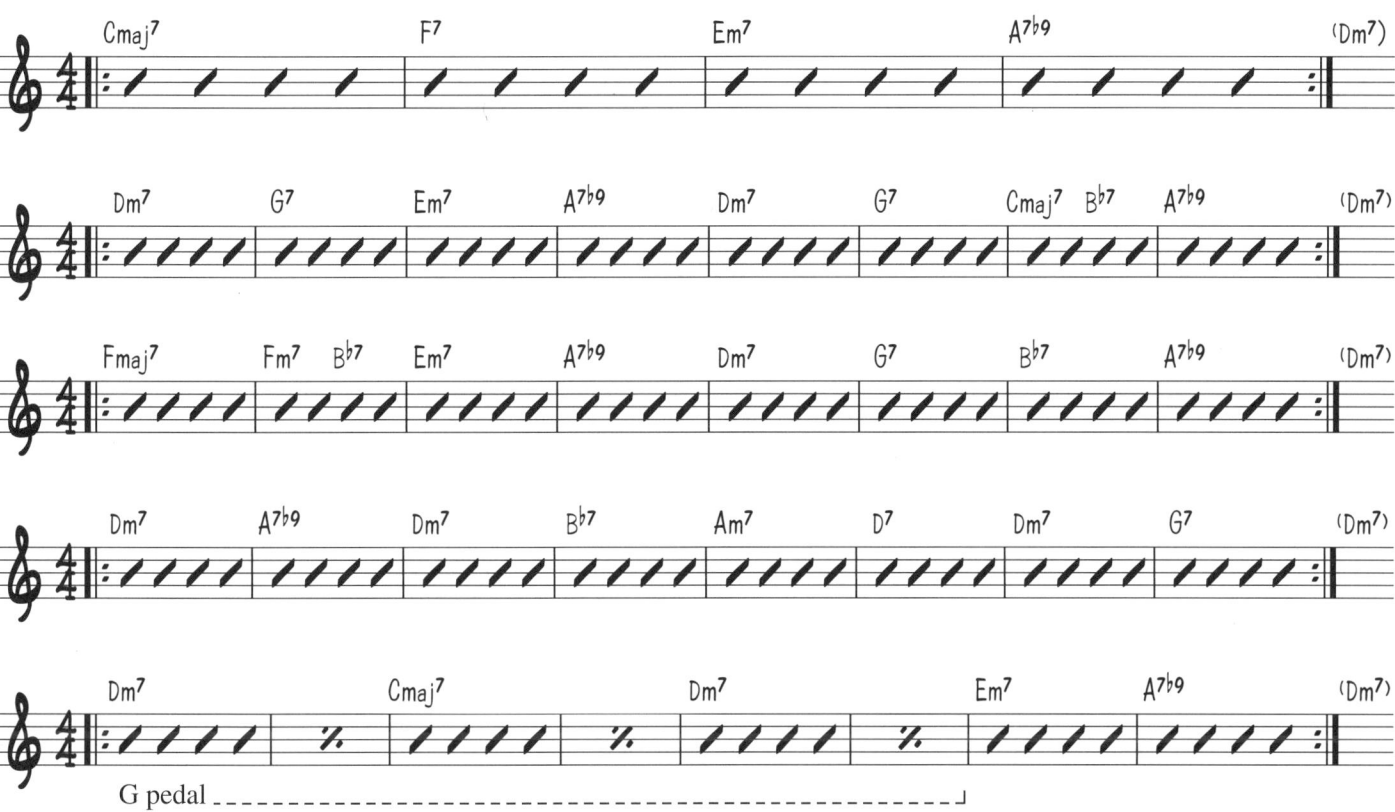

Intros when the first chord in the tune is a IV chord

A few tunes ("Just Friends" and others) begin on the IV chord. An intro for this takes special consideration. Here are a couple of ideas.

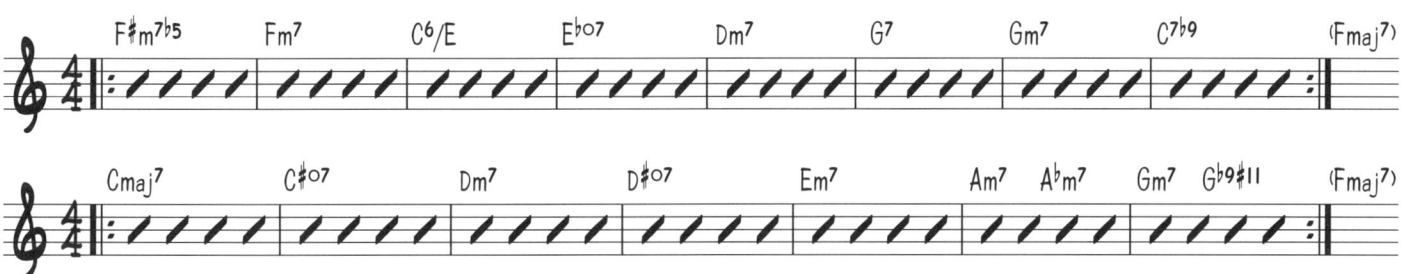

Intros when the first chord in the tune is a I minor chord
I-VI-II-V Intro

Introductions to tunes in a minor key can follow the same type of patterns as for tunes in a major key. The chord qualities need to be adjusted to set up the minor key. These I-VI-II-V intros are just a small sampling of what is possible, but these will be, for the most part, easily described and quickly followed. Repeats are optional.

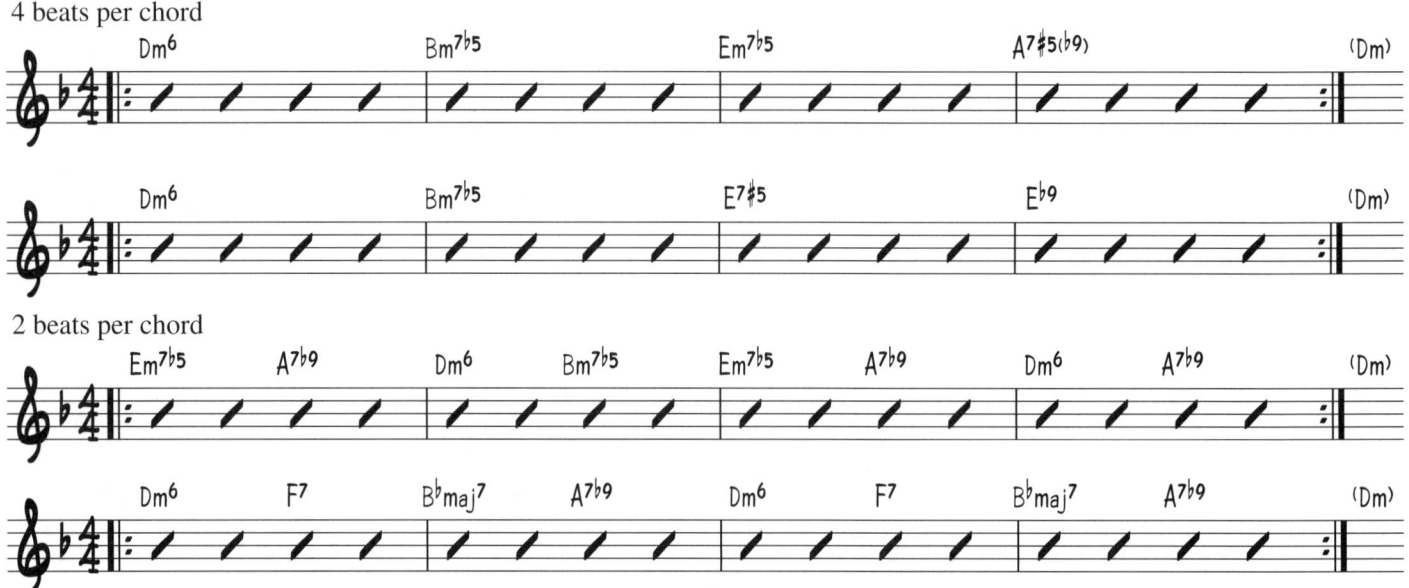

Here are a couple with a pedal on the dominant (V), A in the key of D minor.

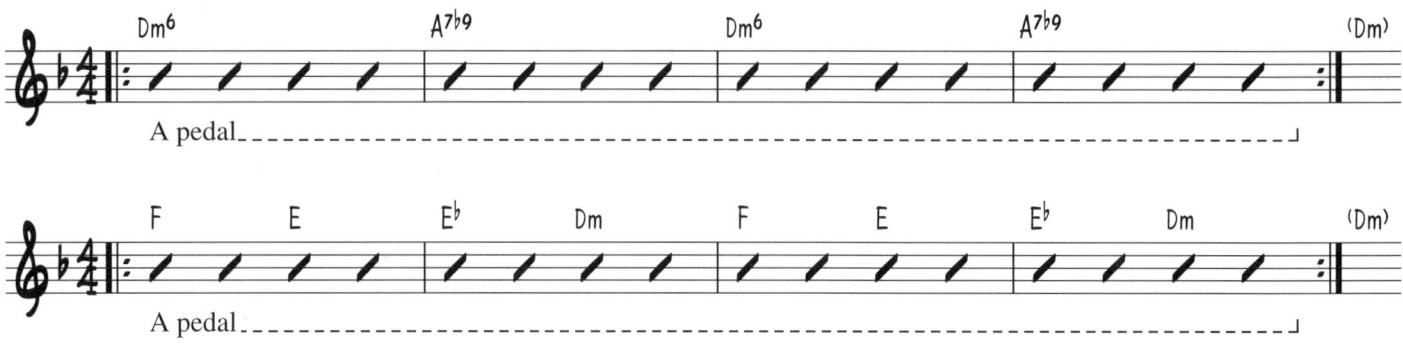

Intros when the first chord in a minor tune is a II chord

Quite a few tunes in a minor key begin on the II chord, which is a m7♭5 chord. Following are a few intros you could use on this type of tune. (Often, an intro for a tune that begins on the I chord will work in this situation.)

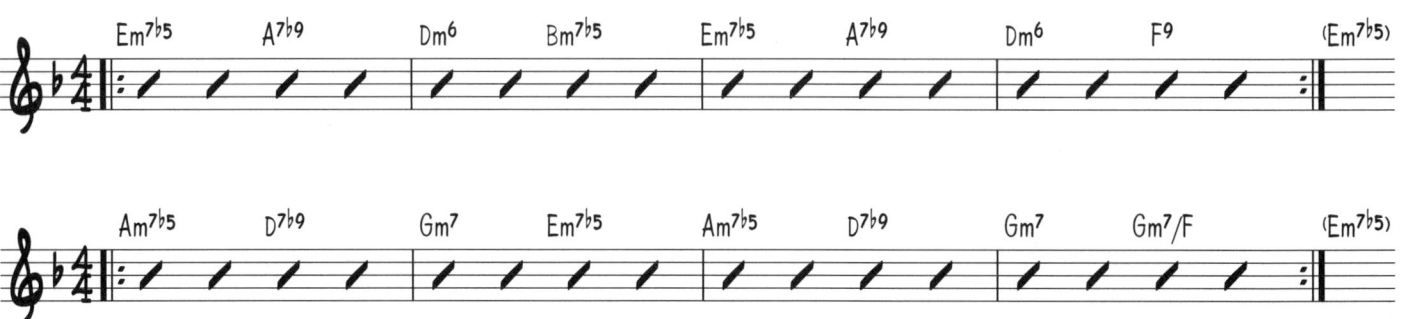

Intros when the first chord in the tune is a IV chord

A few tunes ("Autumn Leaves" and others) begin on the IV chord. An intro for this takes special consideration. Here are a few ideas.

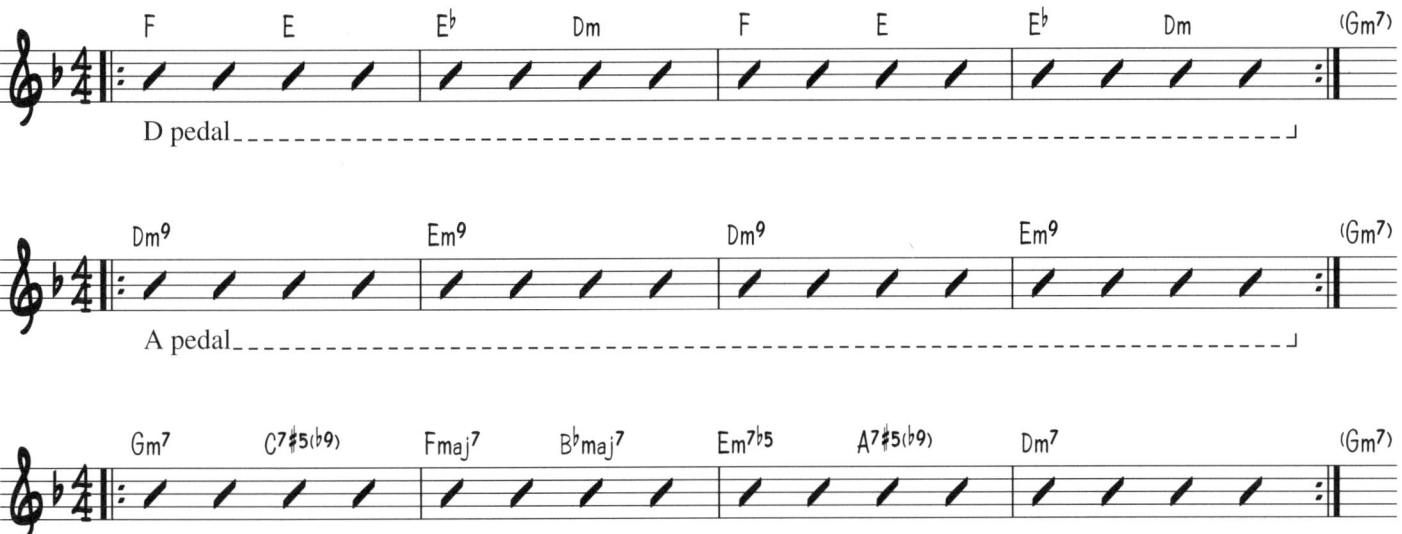

ENDINGS

There are only a few specific endings for specific tunes. Other than these few tunes, endings are usually something that happens spontaneously. Usually the soloist or another musician will take the reins and go in a certain direction, expecting the other musicians to follow along.

The usual exception to this is when a singer is involved. In those cases, the singer is expected to say whether or not they want a tag at the end of a song. The tag usually consists of repeating the final phrase of the song two or three times.

There could be an open vamp of two or four measures at the end of a tune, with someone dictating when the vamp should end or fade out. Normally, at the end of a tag, a final chord or chords are played. An endings vamp is a good opportunity for a soloist to stretch out, since it is only two or four chords to play over.

First we will show you a few endings that could be played starting over the final note of the tune. Then we will present what might happen in a tag, also beginning over the final note. What is appropriate to play in the ending, both melodically and harmonically, depends on what note is played for the final note. It is important to listen to this last note, because it will dictate the direction the ending needs to go. If it is the tonic of the key, usually that means the tune will not have an extended ending. If the last note is one that sounds less "final" – often the 5th or 6th of the key – you will want to extend the ending.

Though we use C major and D minor in the following examples, you should become familiar with these endings in all keys.

Endings with no extensions – Major keys

Here are just a few of the possible endings when it is not extended for a tag or vamp. The ending note is most often the tonic of the key. These written endings begin on that final note.

Extended Endings with Tags or Vamps – Major keys

These are extended endings that include a tag or a vamp. A tag is a repeat of the last phrase of a tune. Usually a tag includes one or two repeats after the initial last phrase. A vamp normally has a two- or four-measure chord progression that is repeated indefinitely with a solo played over it. These written endings begin on the final note of the song proper.

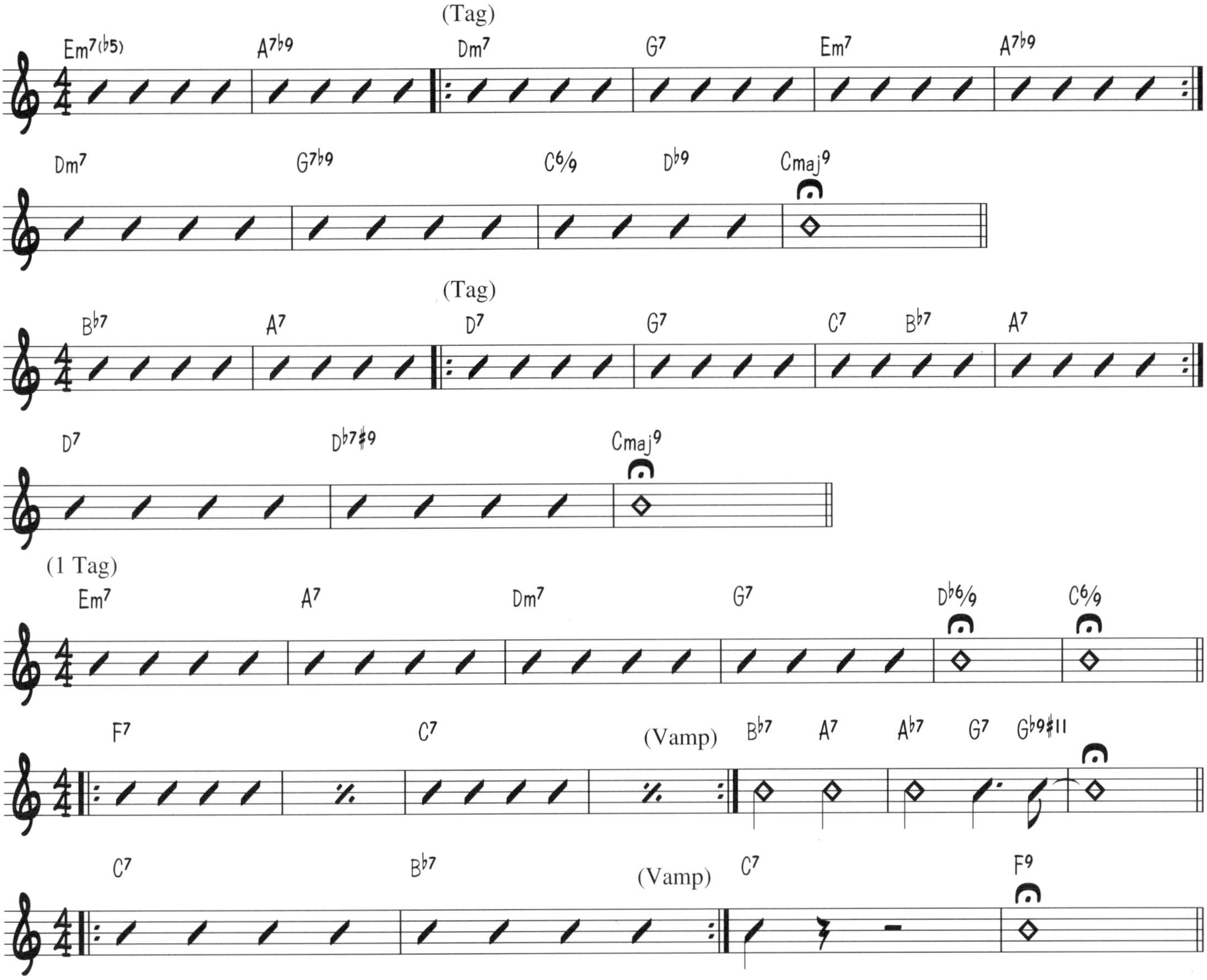

Endings with no extensions – Minor keys

Here are just a few of the possible endings when it is not extended for a tag or vamp. The ending note is most often the tonic of the key. These written endings begin on that final note.

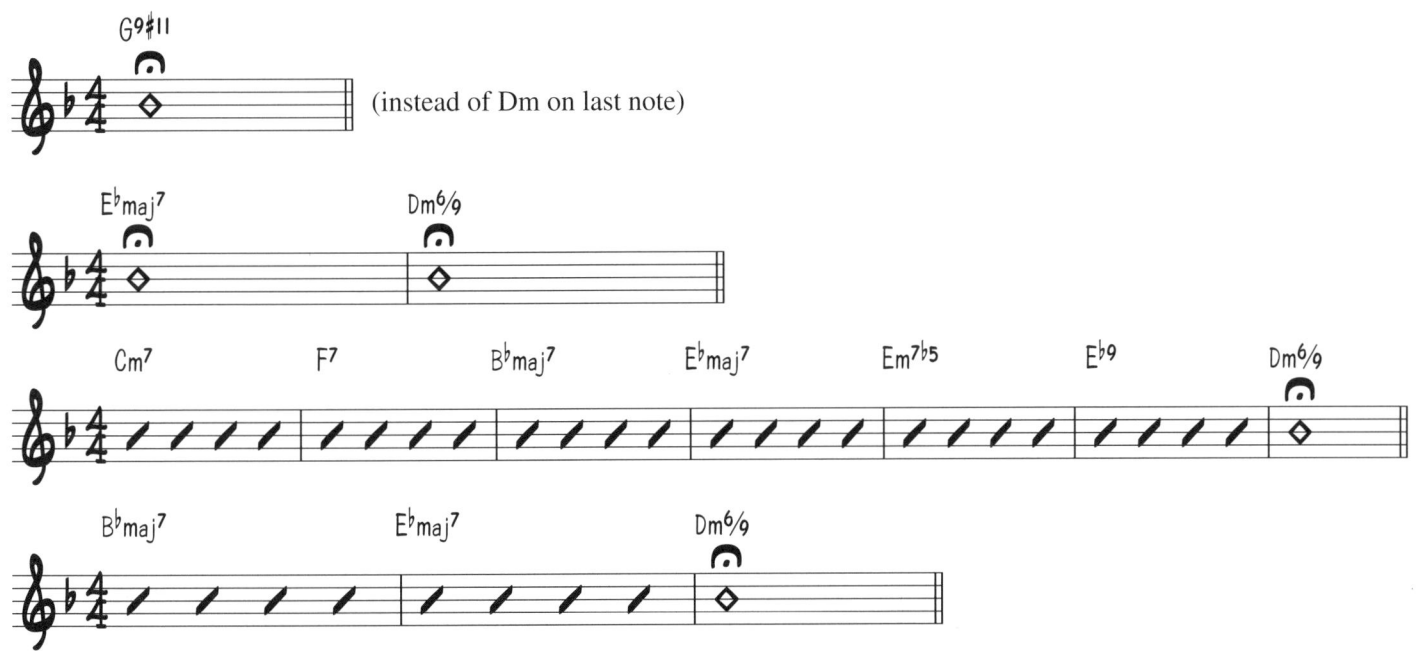

(instead of Dm on last note)

Extended Endings with Tags or Vamps – Minor keys

These are extended endings that include a tag or a vamp. A tag is a repeat of the last phrase of a tune. These written endings begin on the final note of the song proper.

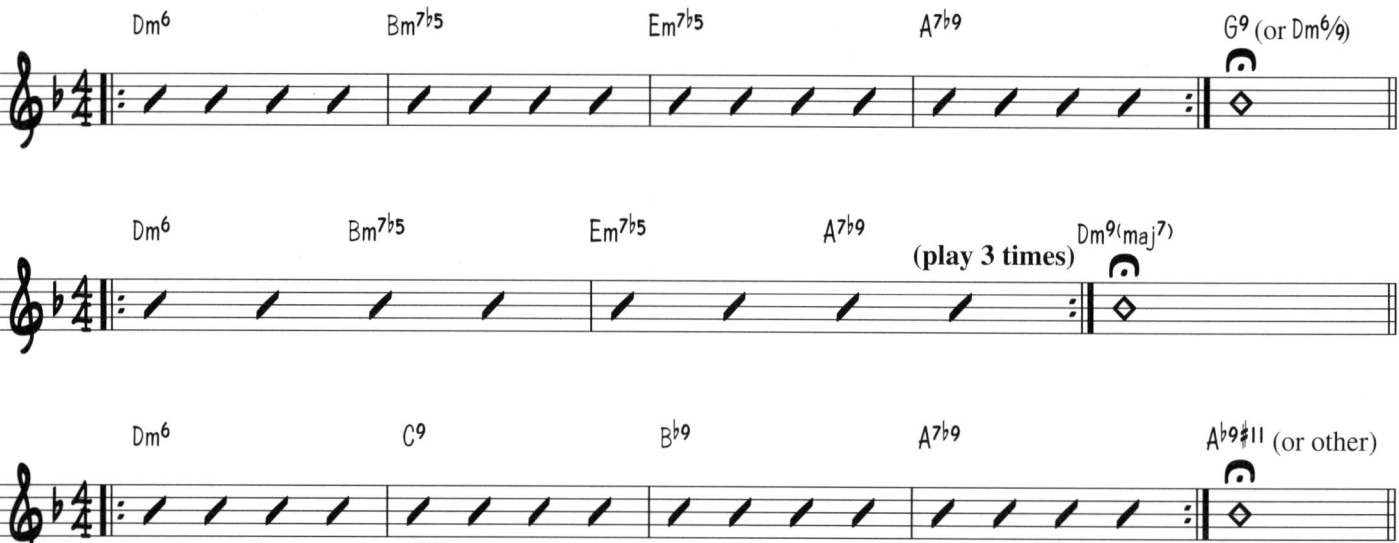

Chapter 7: Practice Suggestions and a Practice Planner

Practice routines vary from teacher to teacher and player to player. Having a regular schedule for practicing will undoubtedly improve your musicianship. Your practicing should include methods of improving technical skills as well as musical creativity. Playing scales and etudes is not enough. You need to expose yourself to unfamiliar harmonic, melodic, and rhythmic ideas.

Any horn player should begin a practice session playing long tones at a medium volume, holding each note until breath is gone. This is the time to foster a steady, pleasant sound. Several minutes of this to begin a practice session is a great idea. Pianists and string players would not do this to improve breath control, but a good and steady sound is great for anyone.

The Practice Planner begins after this long-tone exercise. Next would come the scales. In a one-hour session, five or ten minutes might be right for working on scales, playing from the lowest comfortable note to the highest and back several times. Choose two or three scales to work on for a week. It is useful to play scale notes in a random order to bring a melodic element into this practice. But running the scales up and down is a good way to limber up your fingers (and lip).

Follow this with work on an etude or other piece for improving your technique. Maybe work on a couple at a time. Be very precise in your execution, with a steady tempo and even tone. At first, practice this slowly and then work up to tempo. Many great books are out there for this type of material.

You might want to take a five minute break at this point.

Spend 10 or 15 minutes studying a little theory. Some jazz theory books that I particularly like are *The Jazz Theory Book* by Mark Levine (from Sher Music Co.) and *Alfred's Essentials of Jazz Theory* by Shelly Berg (Alfred Publishing Co., Inc.). You might consider your theory study separate from your actual practicing.

Then spend time playing through some licks. This book has a large section of licks (page 32–51). Reading through transcribed solos is a wonderful way to get a feel for particular players' styles and note choices.

Working on your repertoire would be the next item in your practice session. I once read that Bill Evans learned a new tune every day. This is a wonderful goal to set for yourself.

Find a tune in a fake book and learn it. Learn everything about the tune. Learn the melody and the chord progression. If it is a song, learn the lyric. This will give you great insight into how to interpret the piece, even if simply instrumental.

Also work on more fully-composed music. Expand your knowledge by working on some pieces in another genre of music. Perhaps a classical piece appeals to you. Working on a more extended work will give you a more complete insight into the workings of music.

Last, but not least, spend time playing freely, either on a chord progression or with no structure at all. Let your mind open to any new sounds you might make or hear. The world is full of more musical ideas than any one person will ever absorb. Work on what you like, but be open to new ideas. Your study of this wondrous music called jazz will bring you great joy and fulfillment.

Make copies of the Practice Planner on the following page. Use a three-hole punch and keep them in a ring binder.

I know, this totals out to more than one hour. Indulge yourself. Or save the theory study for a time away from your practice session.

Just as important as the practice and study is listening. Listen closely to musicians you admire and adopt some of their approaches to music. Live performances and recordings are the means musicians have to express their talents. Nowhere is this more vital and fulfilling than in a jam session where new ideas are explored. Listen deeply to the musicians around you in a jam session. This will open your ears and stimulate your musical growth more than just about any other activity.

Best of luck. The study of any music is a path with no end. Jazz offers you more room for individual expression than perhaps any other style. I hope you will find yourself on the bandstand in many jam sessions. It is maybe the best way to learn. Have a great journey!

	PRACTICE PLANNER	
TASK	COMMENTS	TIME
SCALES (Two scales) Formal style and random note choice		5 minutes
ETUDES AND OTHER TECHNICAL PIECES		10 minutes
SHORT BREAK		5 minutes
THEORY STUDY Could be done apart from the practice session		10–15 minutes
LICKS AND TRANSCRIBED SOLOS		10–15 minutes
REPERTOIRE Refining tunes already started and learning new tunes (not more than one per day)		15–20 minutes
RANDOM PLAYING AND EXPLORATIONS (either from chord progressions or unstructured playing, free)		10–15 minutes

chapter 8
50 Frequently Played Tunes – Chord Charts and Online Audio

In order for you to practice your improvising, we've included chord charts for 50 tunes – some of those most frequently played in jam sessions. Melodies are not included, but these can be found in any number of books. The online audio presents several choruses of each of these tunes played by a rhythm section. The charts that follow are based on the recorded audio examples.

Over time, you should add these to your repertoire. A second list of tunes often played at jam sessions is given on page 65. Learn all the tunes on both lists.

Have fun!

Chord Charts for Tunes on the Play-Along Online Audio Tracks

66	All of Me	98	Just Friends
67	All the Things You Are	95	Killer Joe
68	Alone Together	100	Like Someone in Love
69	Autumn Leaves	101	Love Is Here to Stay
70	Body and Soul	102	Maiden Voyage
71	Bye Bye Blackbird	103	Mr. P.C.
72	Cantaloupe Island	104	Misty
74	Caravan	105	My Funny Valentine
73	Cherokee (Indian Love Song)	106	Nica's Dream
76	Days of Wine and Roses	108	Night and Day
78	Don't Get Around Much Anymore	110	A Night in Tunisia
80	Doxy	112	On Green Dolphin Street
81	Footprints	113	One Note Samba
82	Four	114	Perdido
83	The Girl from Ipanema	116	Secret Love
84	Have You Met Miss Jones?	115	So What
85	Honeysuckle Rose	118	Softly As in a Morning Sunrise
86	How About You?	120	Speak Low
88	How High the Moon	119	Star Eyes
90	I Got Rhythm	122	Stella by Starlight
89	I'll Remember April	123	Take the "A" Train
92	I'm Old Fashioned	124	Tangerine
93	In a Mellow Tone	125	Things Ain't What They Used to Be
94	In a Sentimental Mood	126	Wave
96	It's You or No One	127	Yardbird Suite

Additional tunes that should be familiar to players in jam sessions

Angel Eyes	My Little Suede Shoes
Au Privave	My Romance
Bag's Groove	My Shining Hour
Beautiful Love	Now's The Time
Billie's Bounce	Oleo
Black Orpheus	Out of Nowhere
Blue Bossa	Povo
Blue Monk	Recorda Me
Bolivia	'Round Midnight
Broadway	Scrapple from the Apple
Ceora	Seven Steps to Heaven
Con Alma	Solar
Confirmation	Song for My Father
East of the Sun	The Song Is You
Freedom Jazz Dance	Stablemates
The Gentle Rain	Straight, No Chaser
Groovin' High	Summertime
How Insensitive	There Is No Greater Love
I Remember You	There Will Never Be Another You
If I Were a Bell	Tune-Up
In Your Own Sweet Way	Undecided
Jitterbug Waltz	Up Jumped Spring
Limehouse Blues	Watermelon Man
Lover	Well You Needn't
Minority	When Sunny Gets Blue
Misty	Whisper Not
Moanin'	Will You Still Be Mine?
Moment's Notice	Woody'n You
Morning	Yardbird Suite

All of Me

—Seymour Simons/Gerald Marks

All the Things You Are

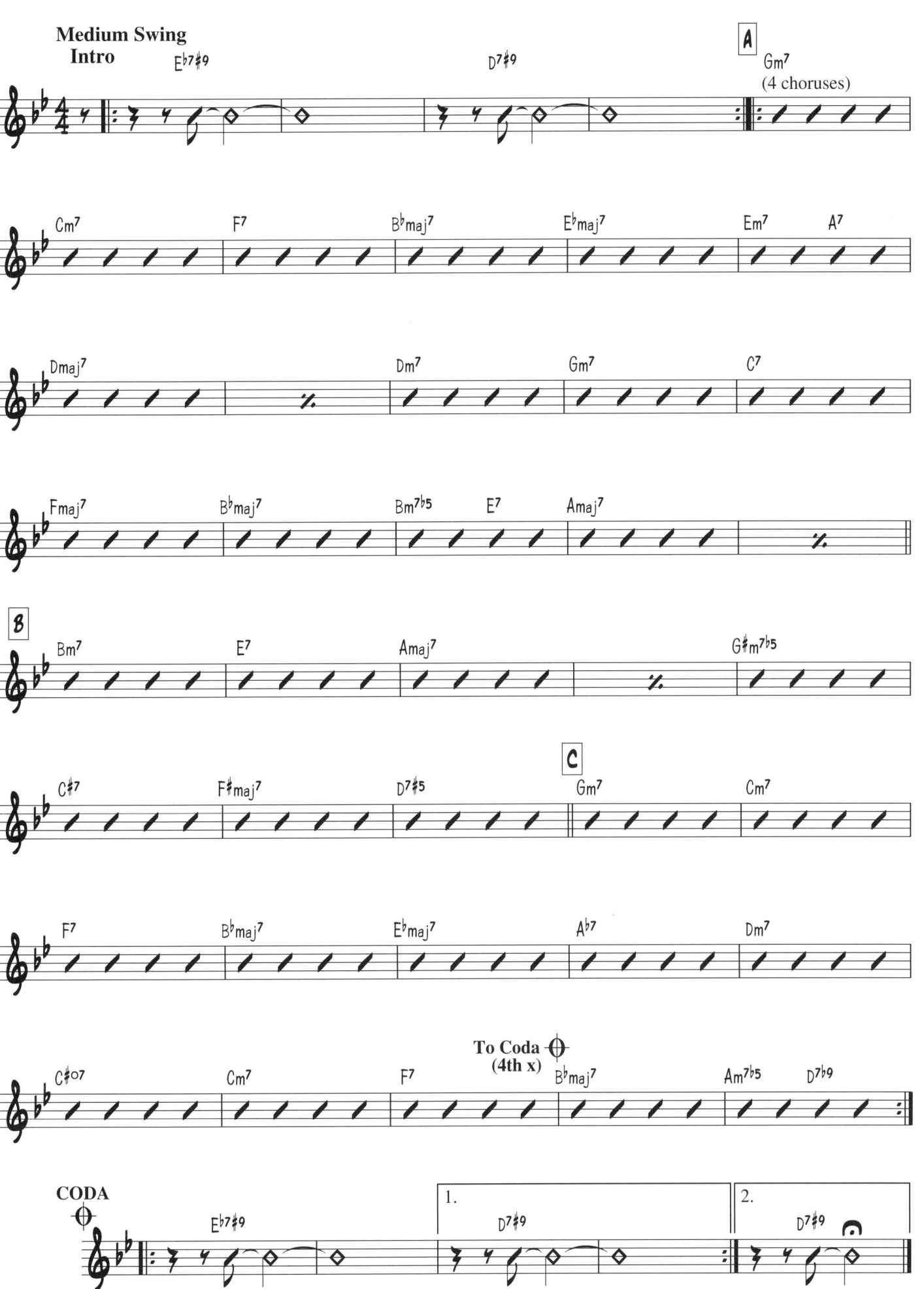

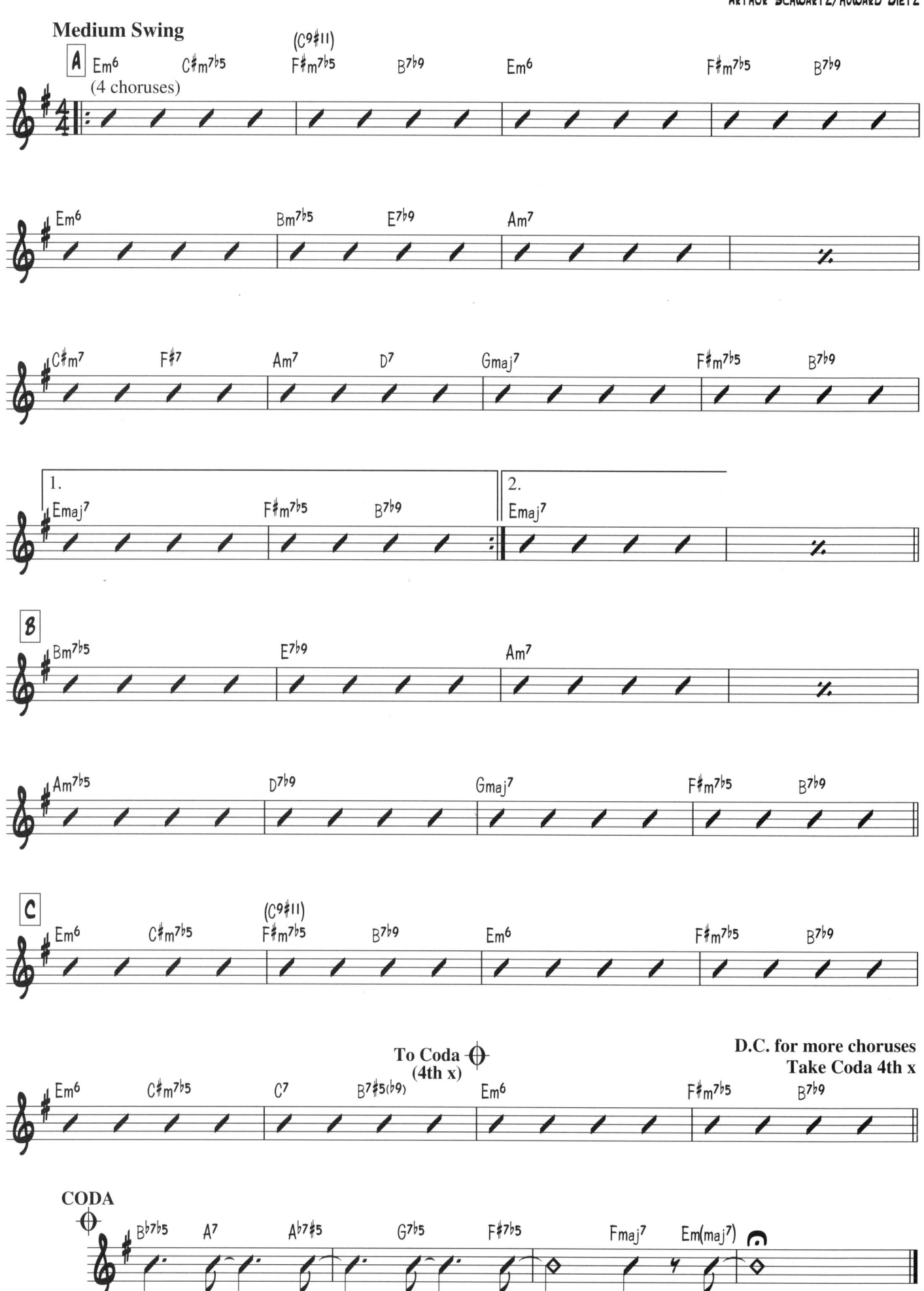

Autumn Leaves

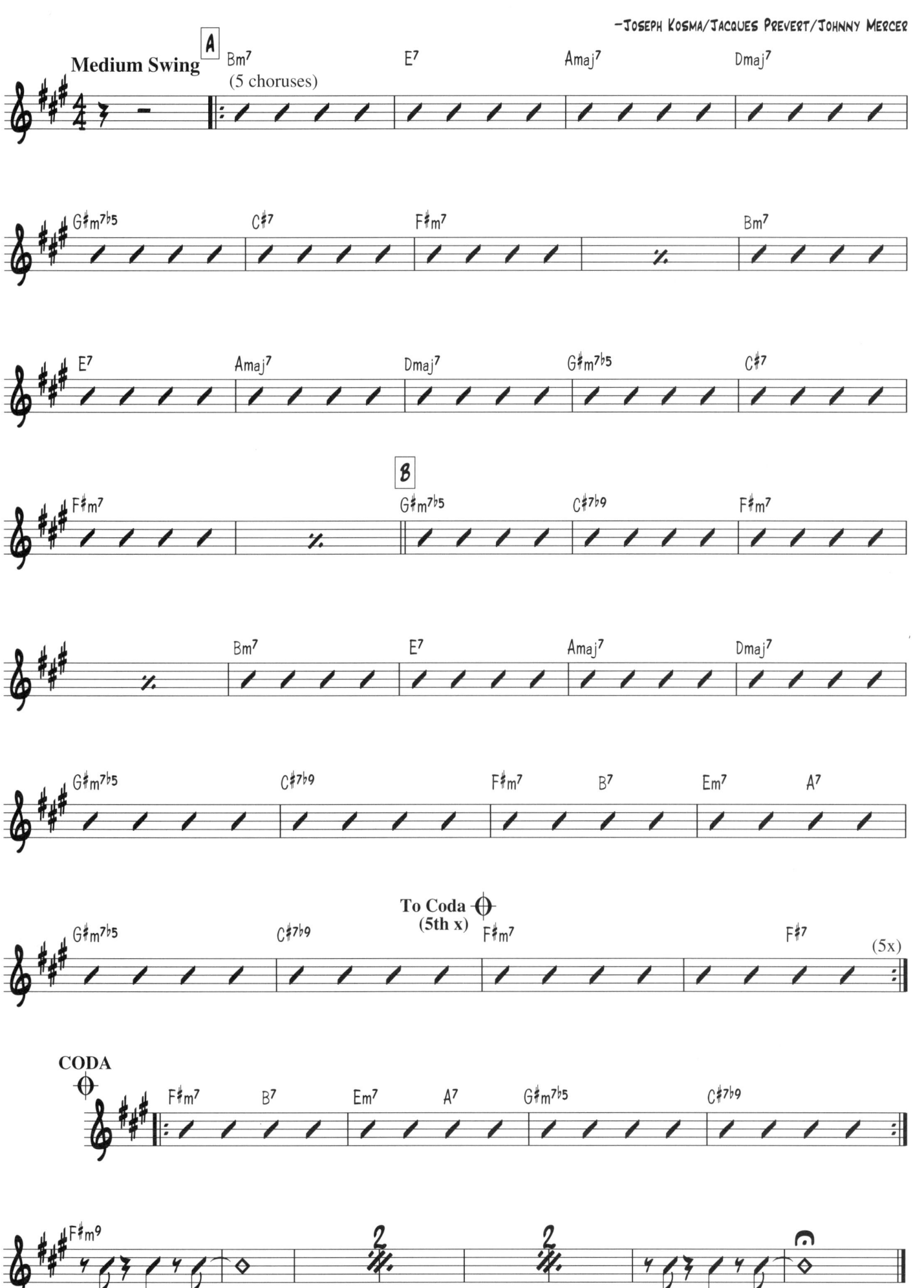

Body and Soul

—Johnny Green/Edward Heyman/Robert Sour/Frank Eyton

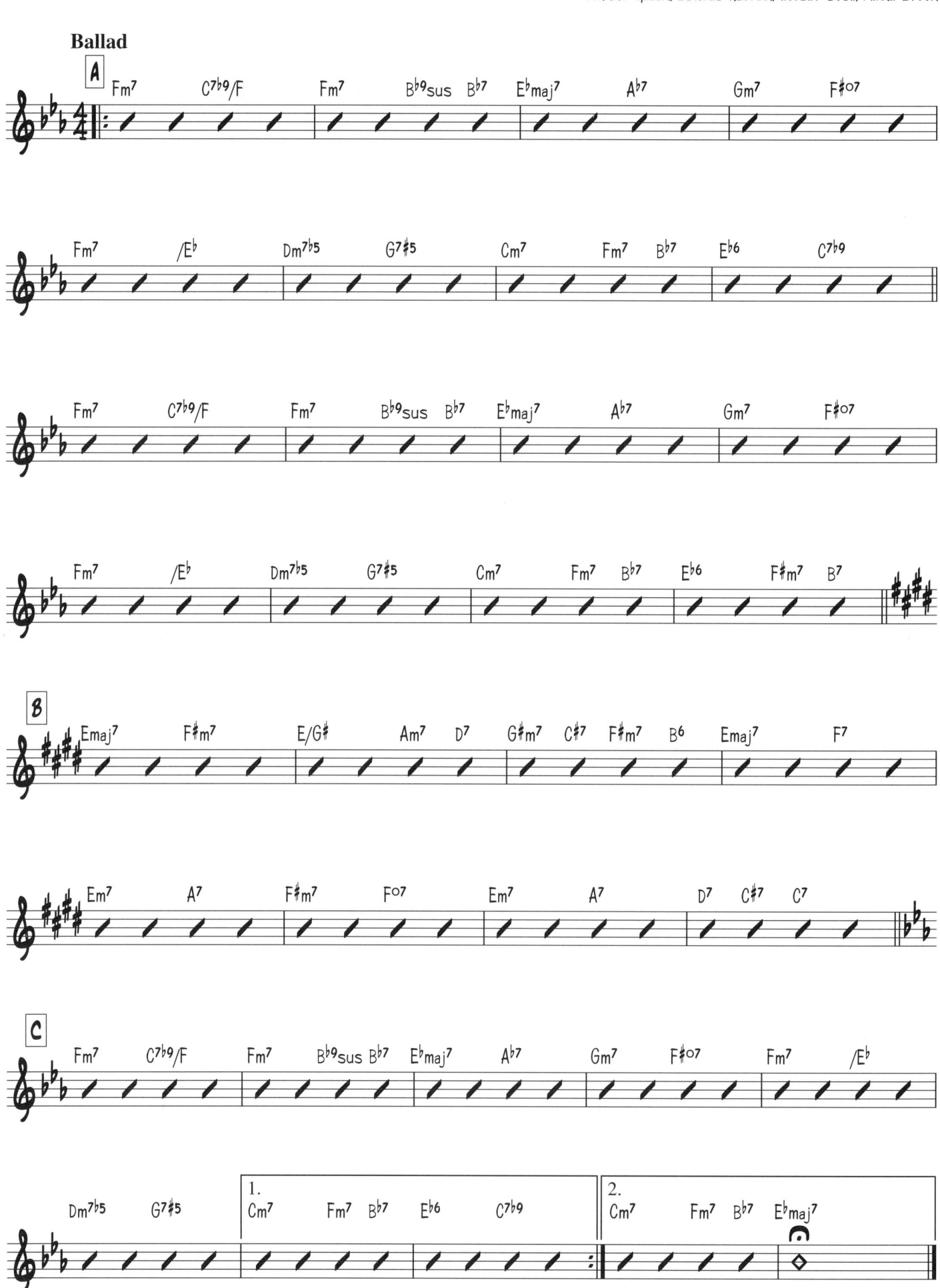

Bye Bye Blackbird

—Ray Henderson/Mort Dixon

Cantaloupe Island

—Herbie Hancock

Caravan

—Duke Ellington/Irving Mills/Juan Tizol

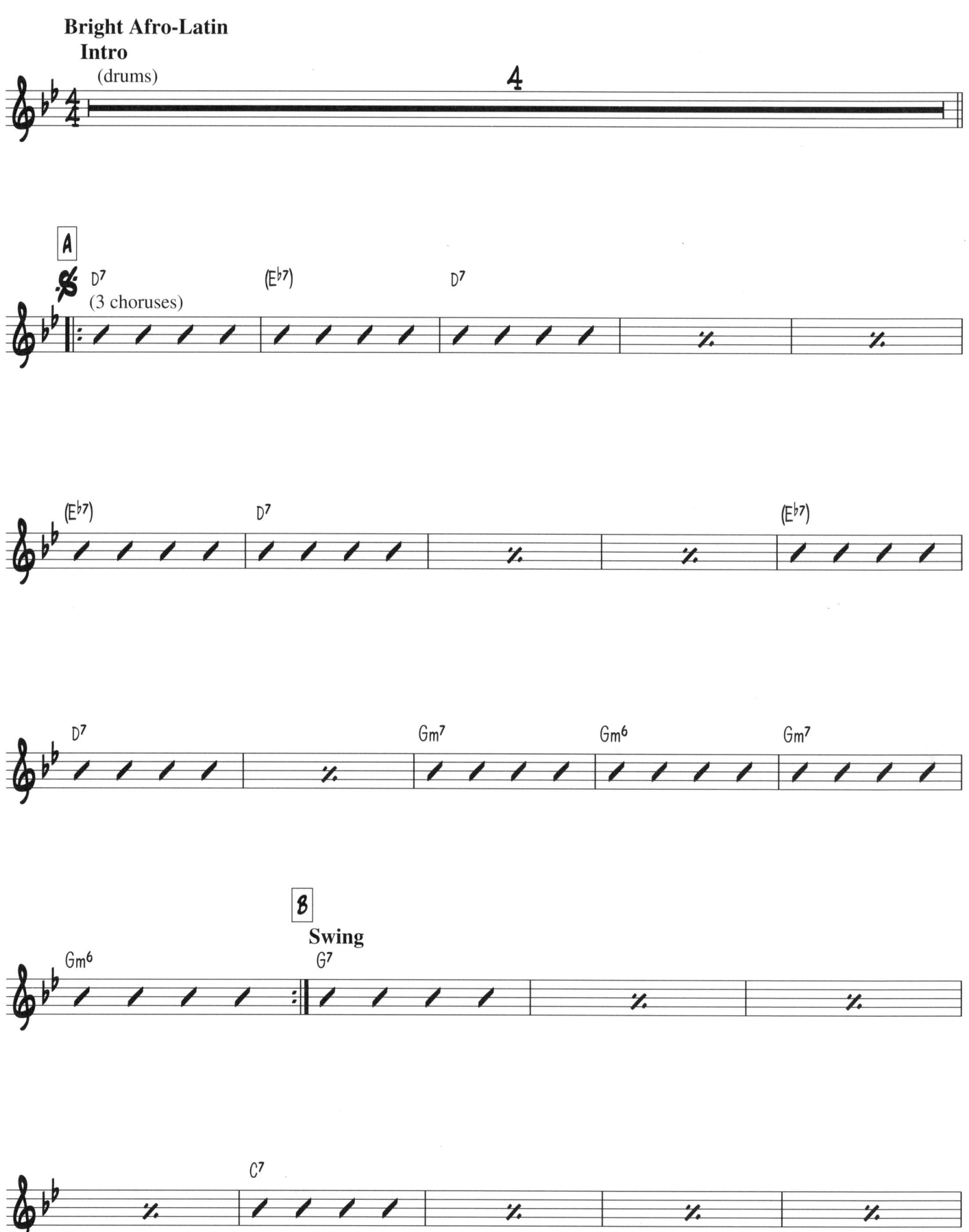

Solos may swing throughout.

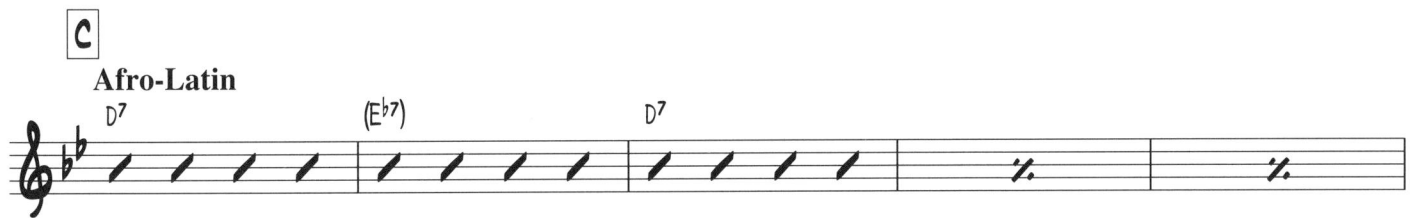

Afro-Latin

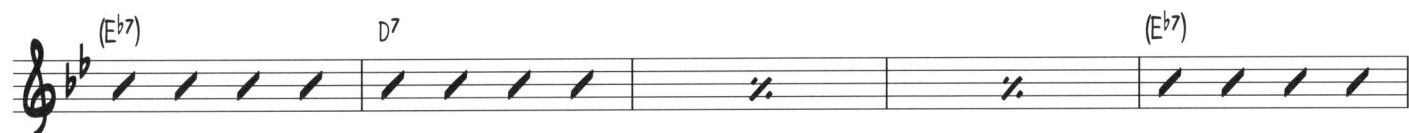

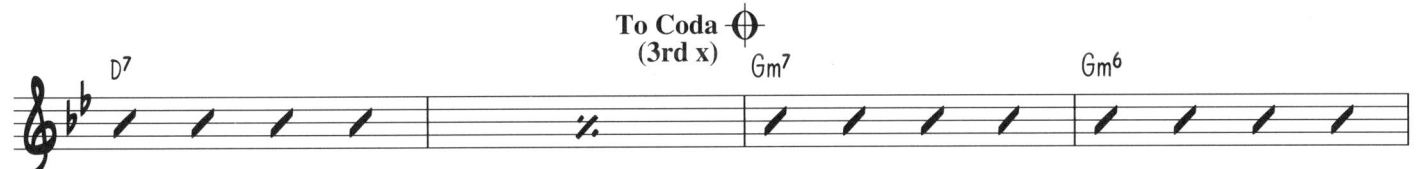

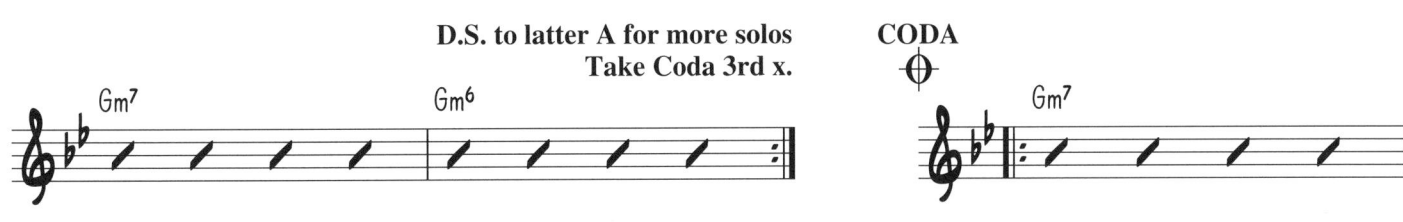

Days of Wine and Roses

—Henry Mancini/Johnny Mercer

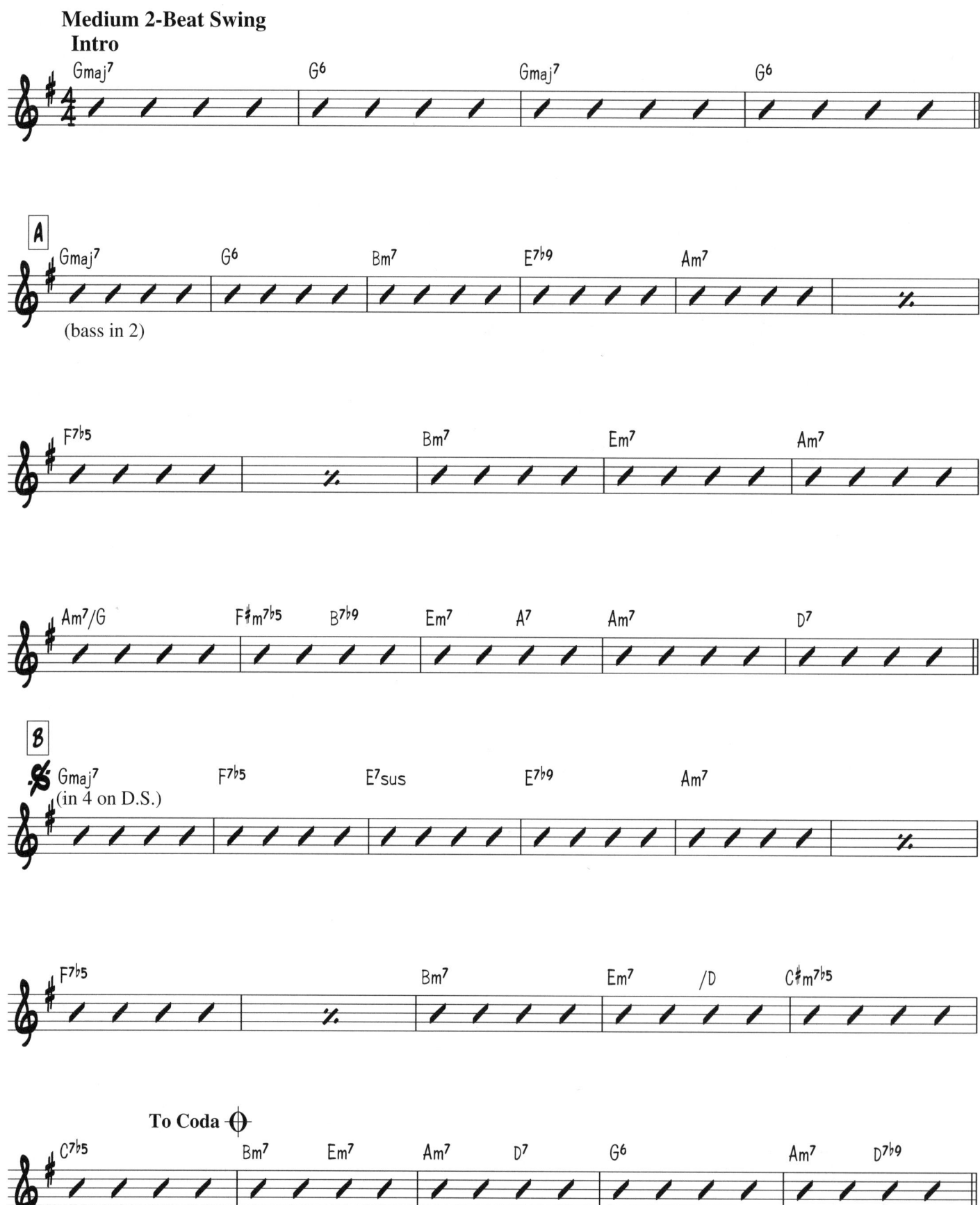

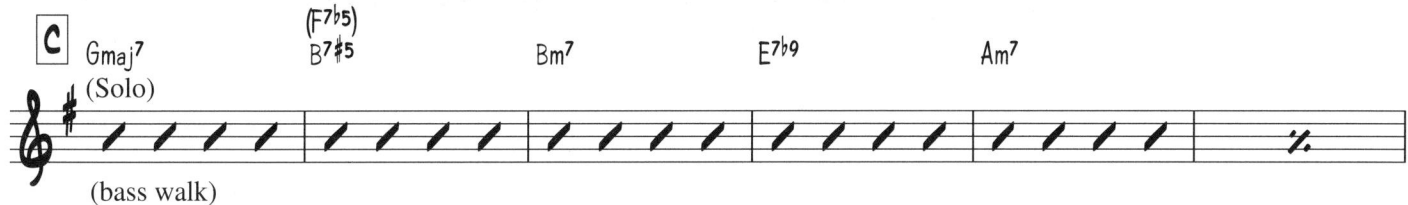

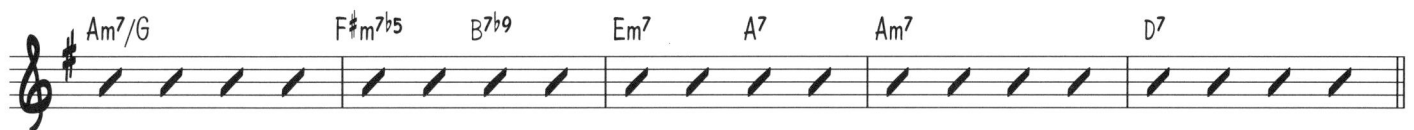

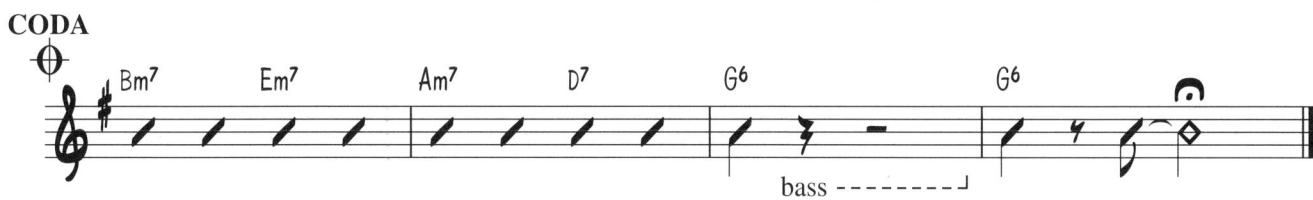

Don't Get Around Much Anymore

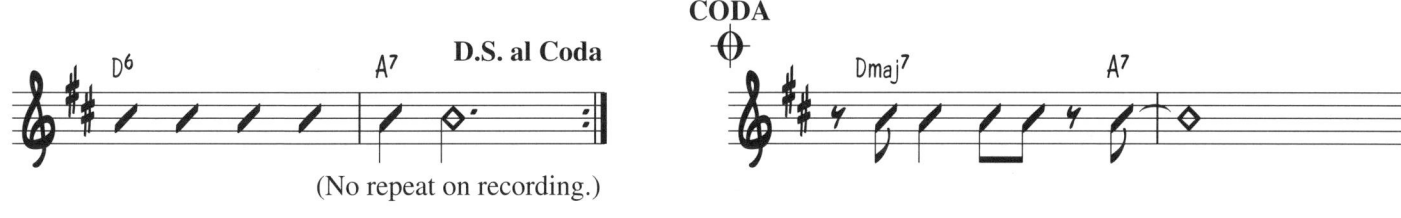

(No repeat on recording.)

Doxy

—Sonny Rollins

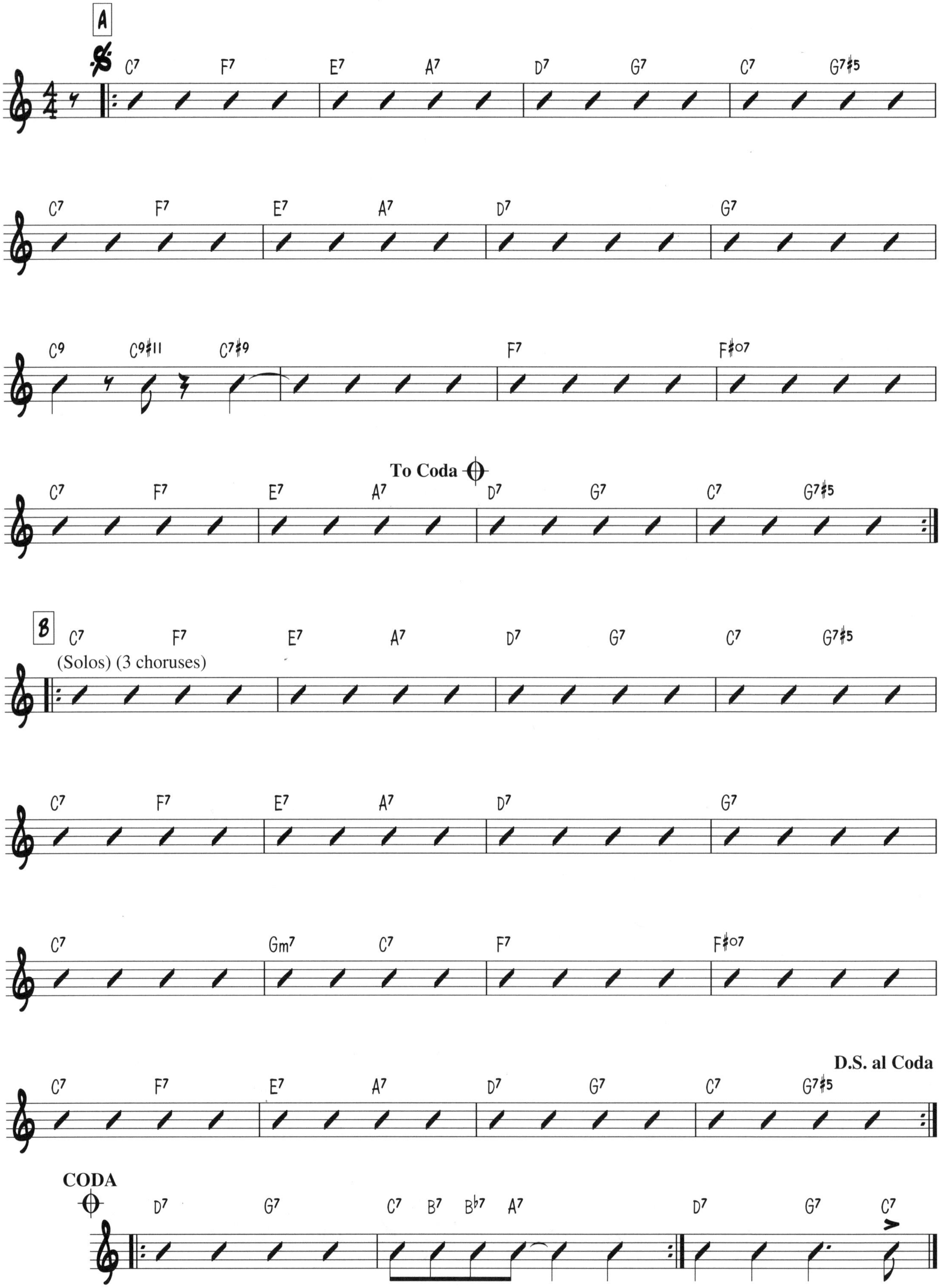

FOOTPRINTS

—Wayne Shorter

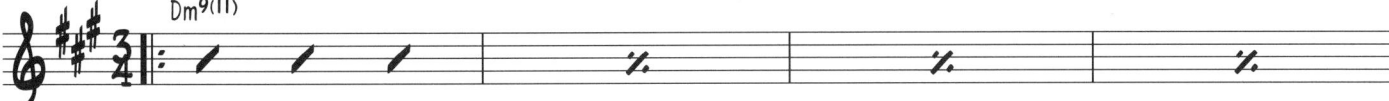

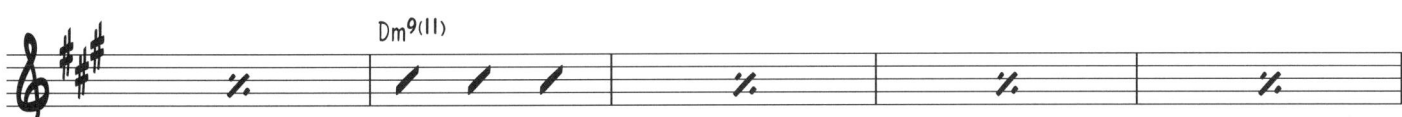
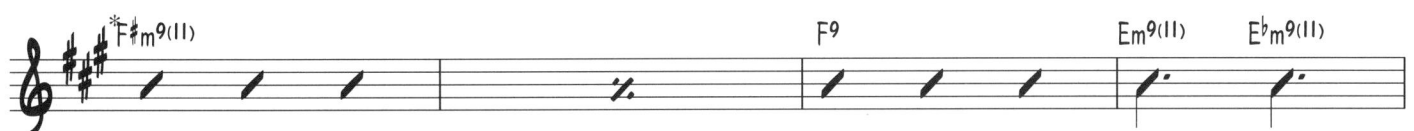
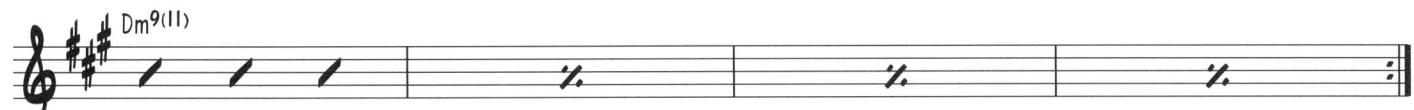

* Variations on bars 17–20 of letter A.

Four

—Miles Davis

The Girl From Ipanema
(Garôta de Ipanema)

—Antonio Carlos Jobim/Vinicius de Moraes/Norman Gimbel

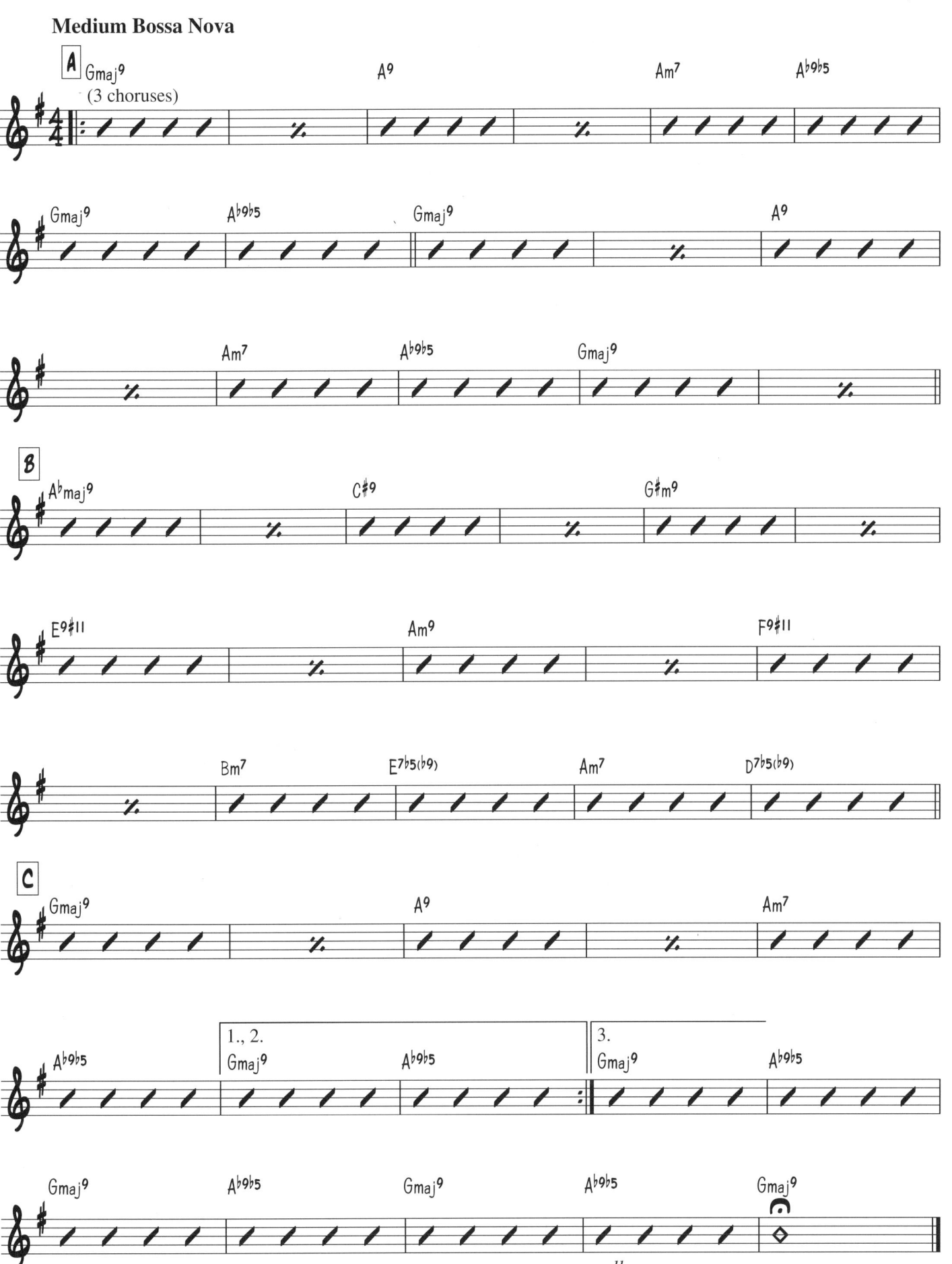

Have You Met Miss Jones?

—Richard Rodgers/Lorenz Hart

Medium

A | Gmaj7 | Bm7 | E7 | Am7 | D7 |
(5 choruses)

| Bm7 | Em7 | Am7 | D7b9 |

| Gmaj7 | Bm7 | E7 | Am7 | D7 |

| Bm7 | Em7 | Dm7 | G7b9 |

B | Cmaj7 | Bbm7 | Eb7 | Abmaj7 | F#m7 | B7 |

| Emaj7 | Bbm7 | Eb7 | Abmaj7 | Am7 | D7b9 |

C | Gmaj7 | Bm7 | E7 | Am7 | D7 | C7 | **To Coda** (5th x)

1. | Bm7 | E7b9 | Am7 | D7b9 | G6 | (solo break) | (Am7 | D7b9) |

2.–4. | Bm7 | E7b9 | Am7 | D7b9 | G6 | Am7 | D7b9 |
Repeat for more solos, Take Coda 5th x

CODA | Bm7 | E7b9 | Am7 | D7b9 | G6 | G6/9 |

Honeysuckle Rose

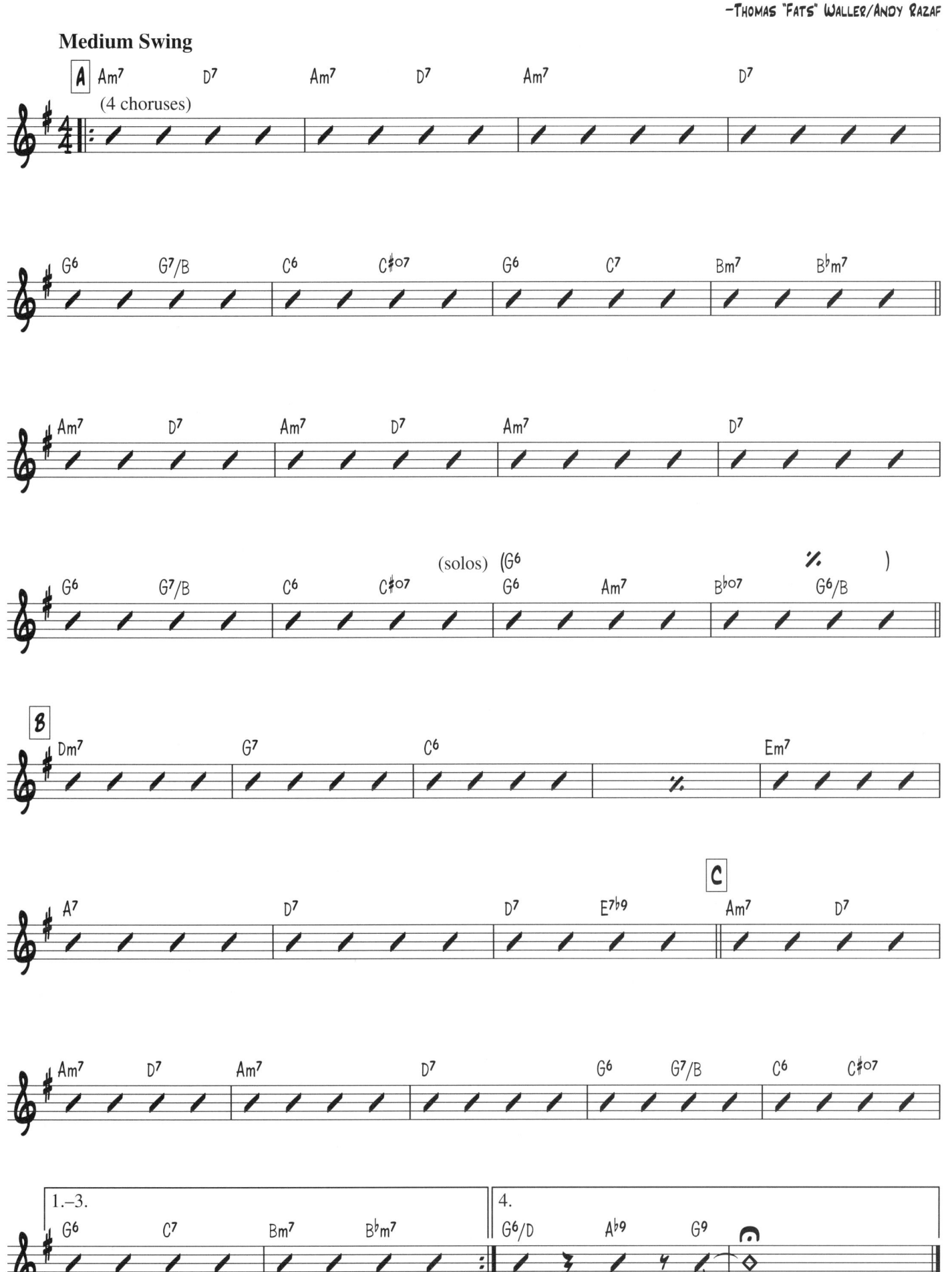

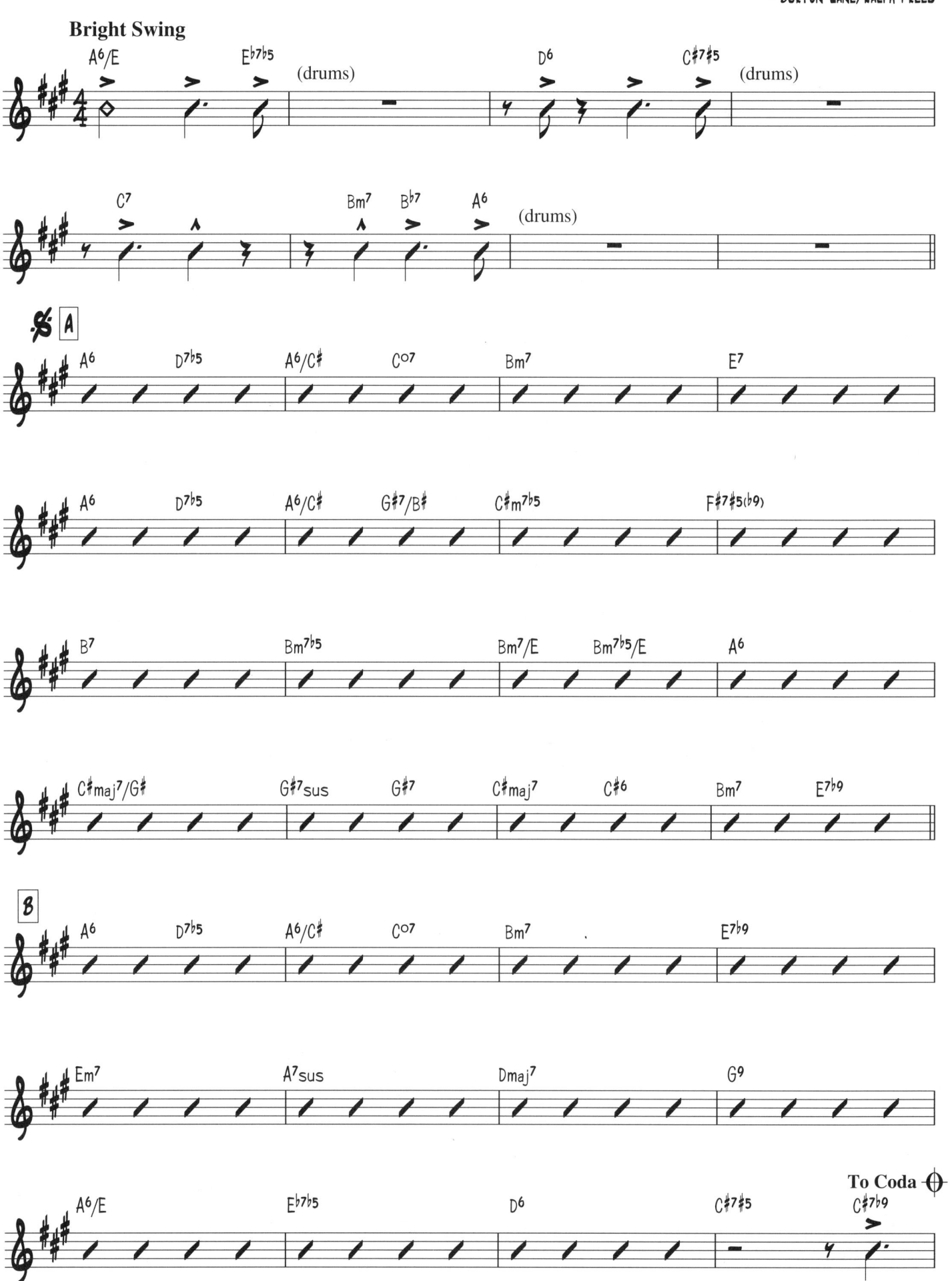

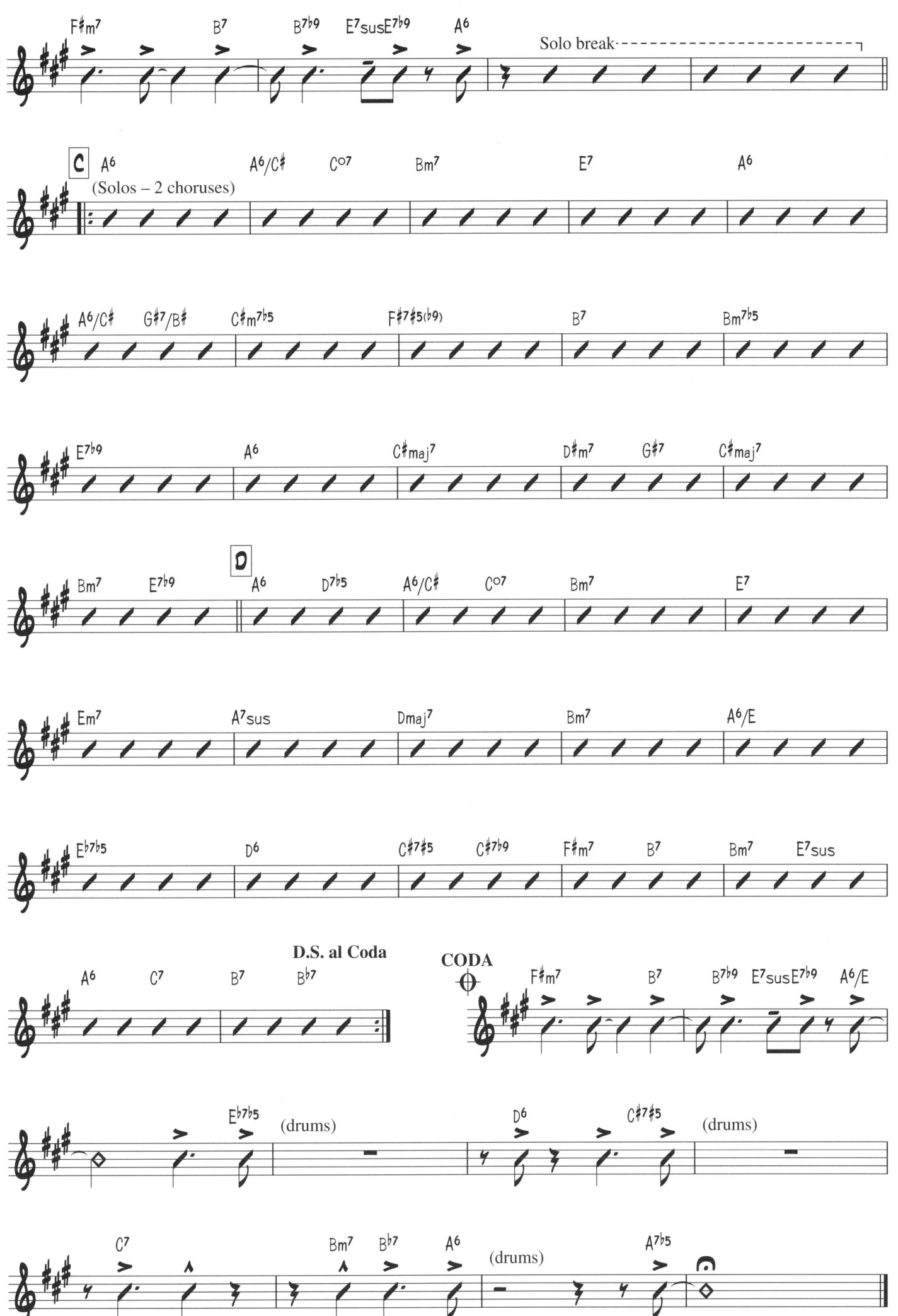

How High the Moon

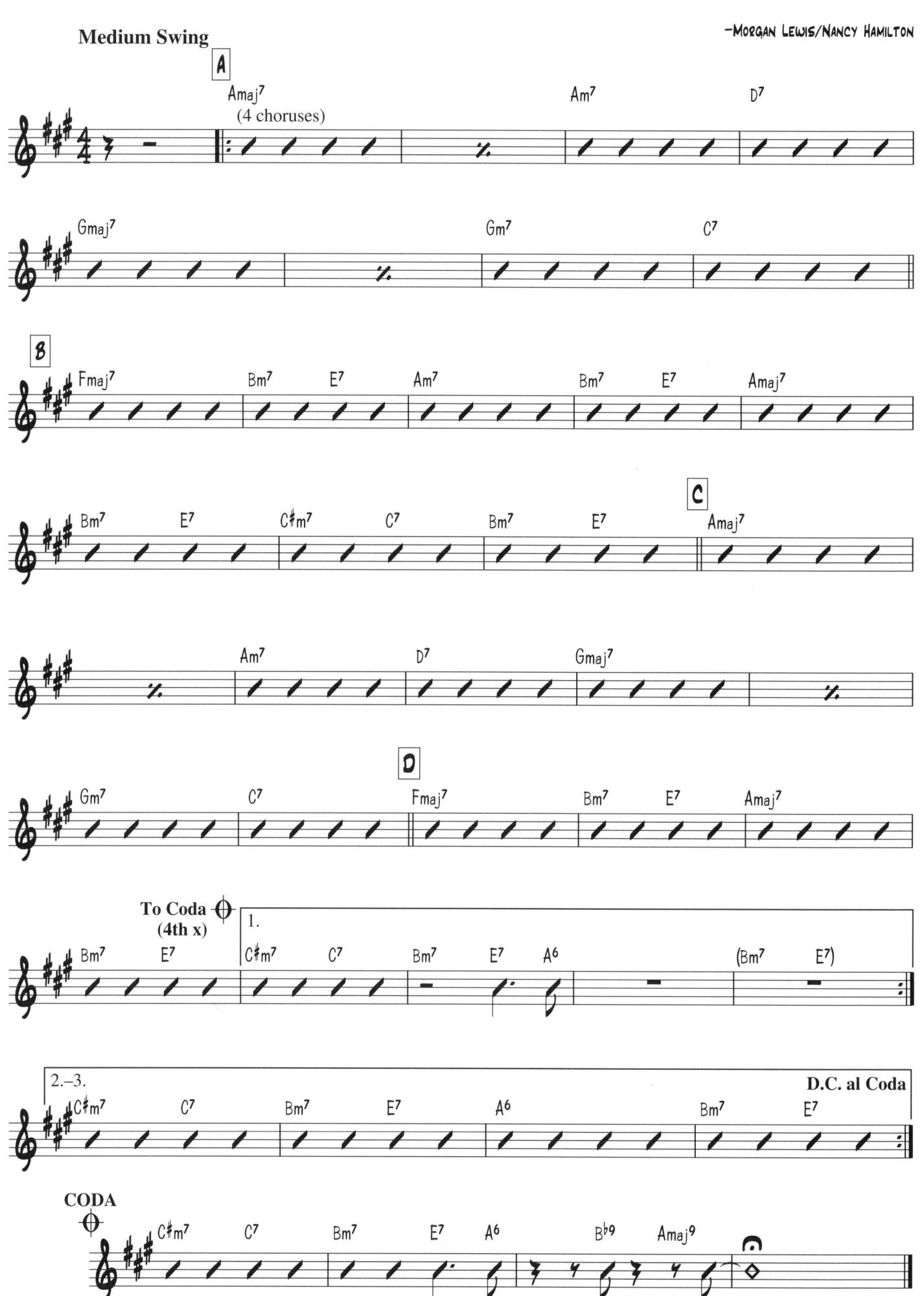

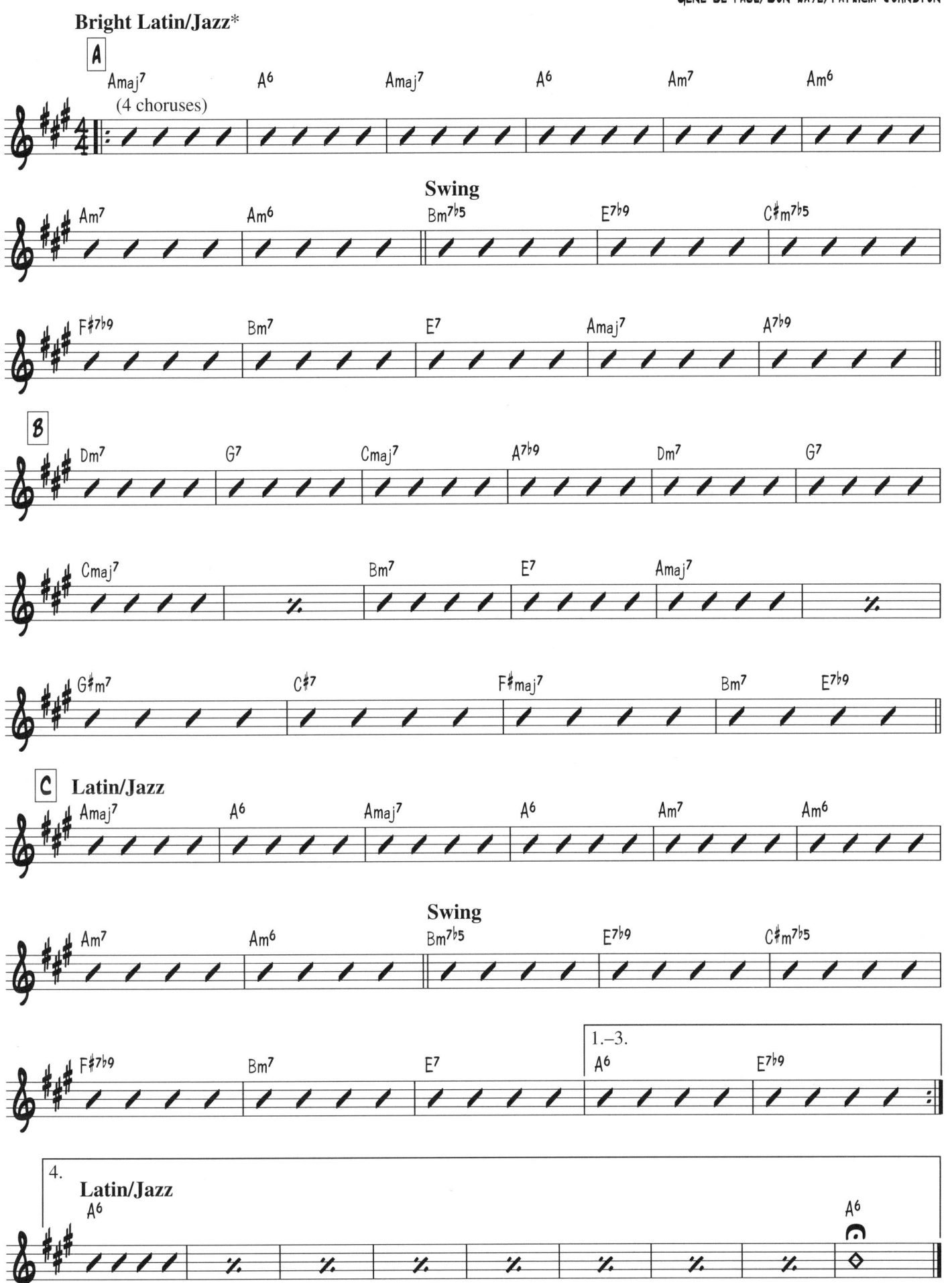

I Got Rhythm

—George Gershwin/Ira Gershwin

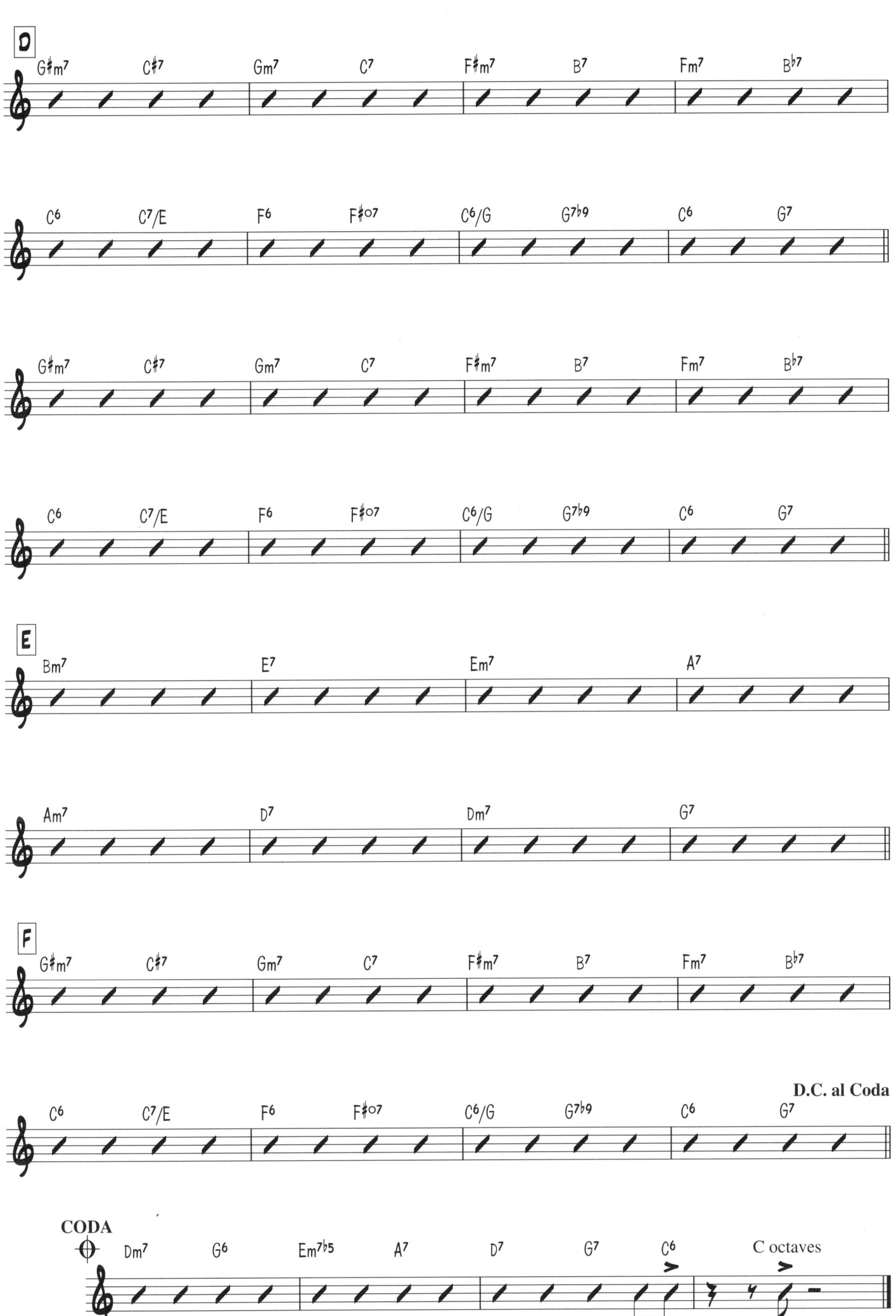

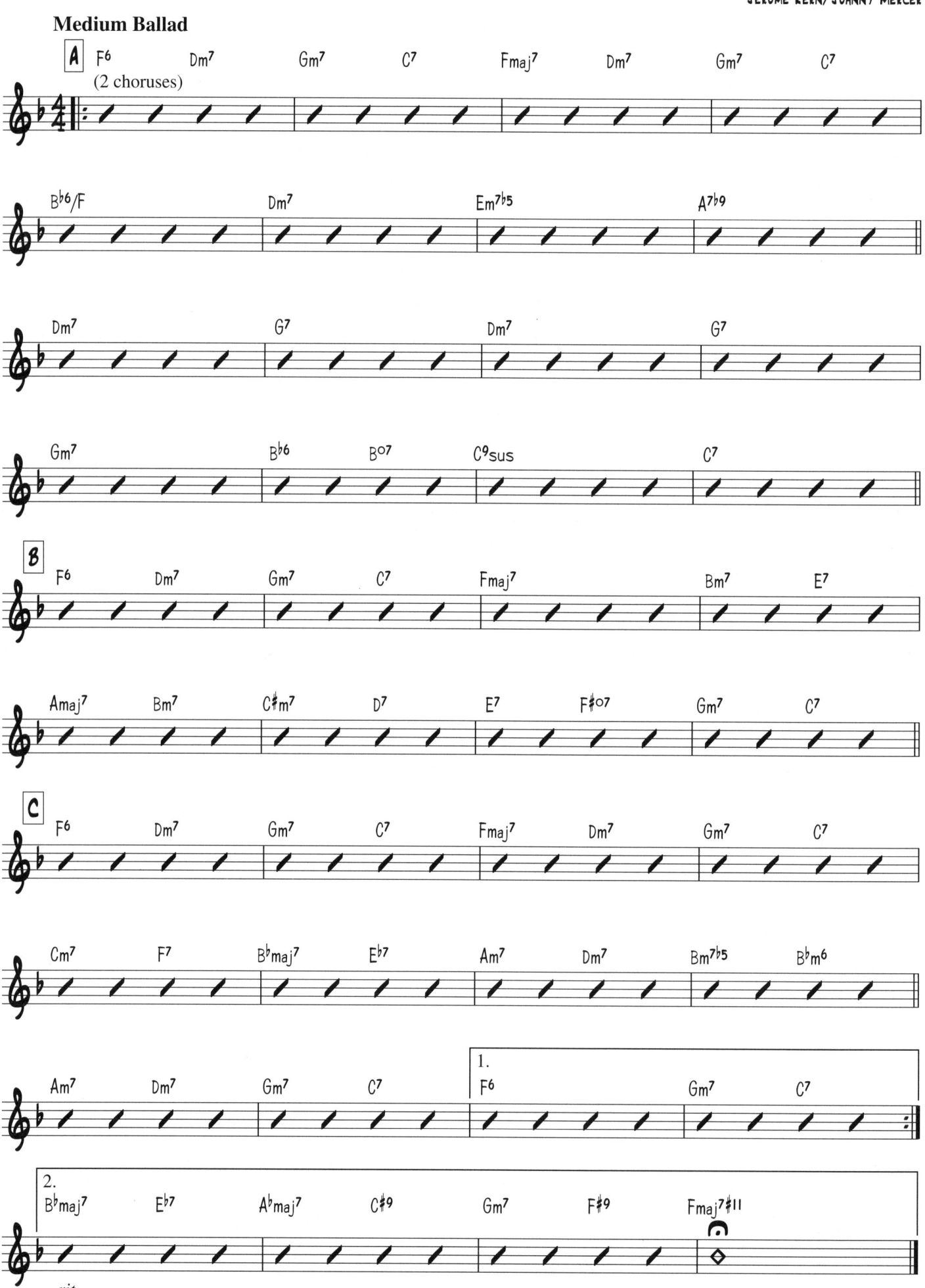

In a Mellow Tone

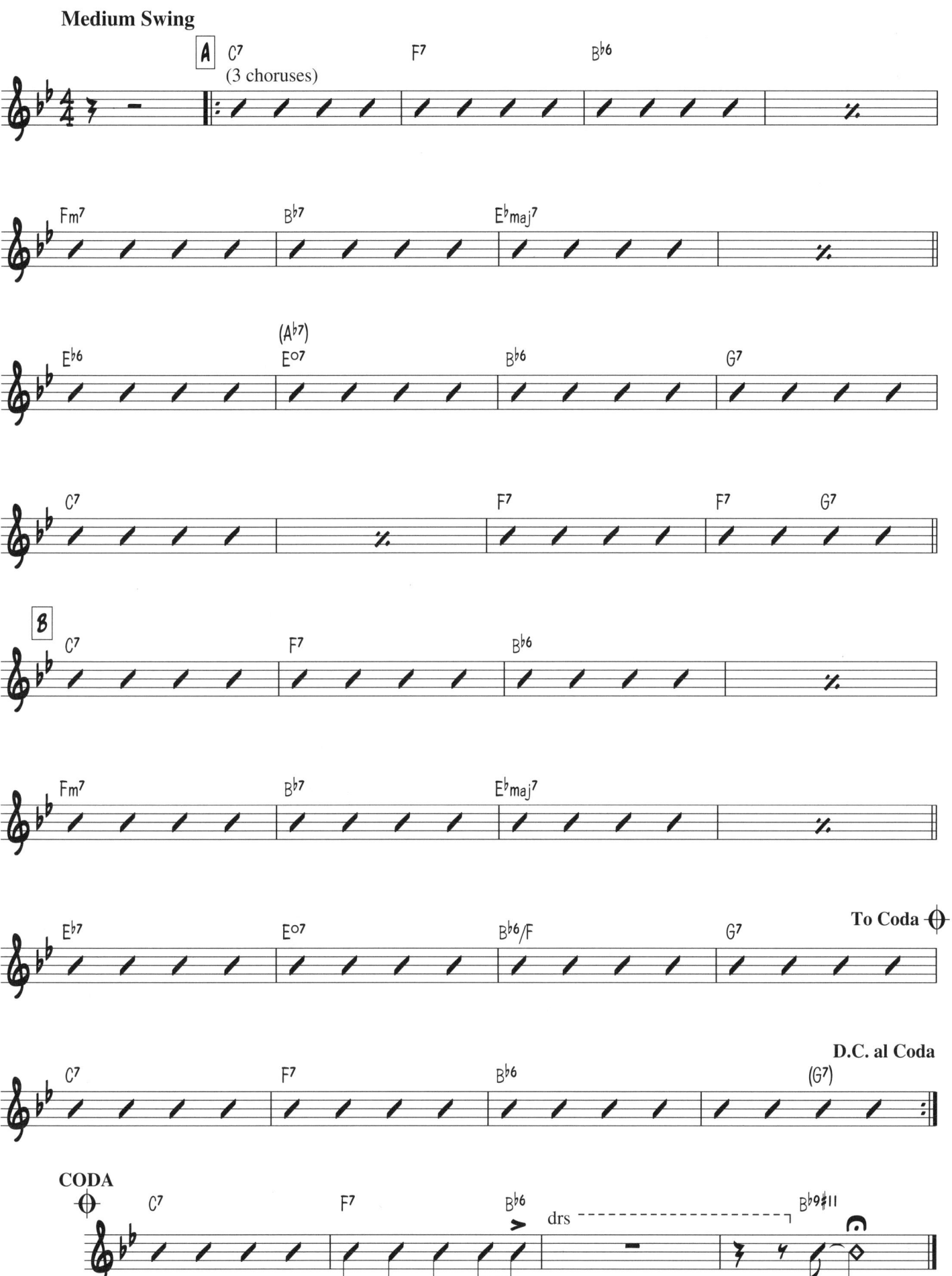

In a Sentimental Mood

—Duke Ellington/Irving Mills/Manny Kurtz

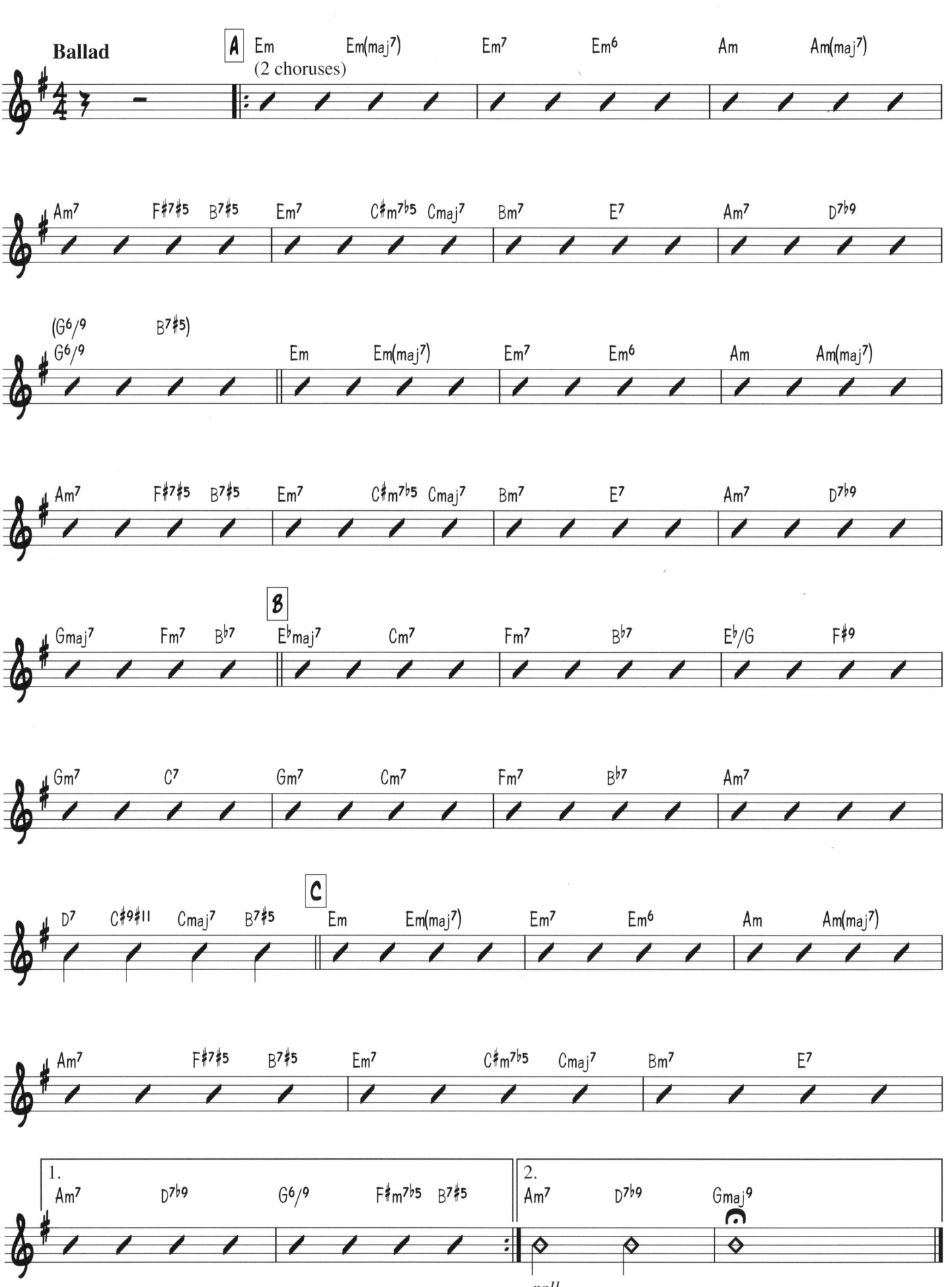

Killer Joe

—Benny Golson

Medium Swing

| D7 | C7 | D7 | C7 |

solo walking bass- -

A (4 choruses)

D7	C7	D7	C7
D7	C7	D7	C7
D7	C7	D7	C7
D7	C7	D7	C7

B (half-time feel)

| F#m7b5 | B7b9 | Fm7 | Bb9   Bbb7b9 |

| B7 | Bb9sus   Bb7 | F#m7 | B7b9 |

C (original feel)

| D7 | C7 | D7 | C7 |
| D7 | C7 | D7 | C7 | (4 x)

TAG

| D7 | C7 | D7 | C7 | D7 |

95

It's You or No One

—Jule Styne/Sammy Cahn

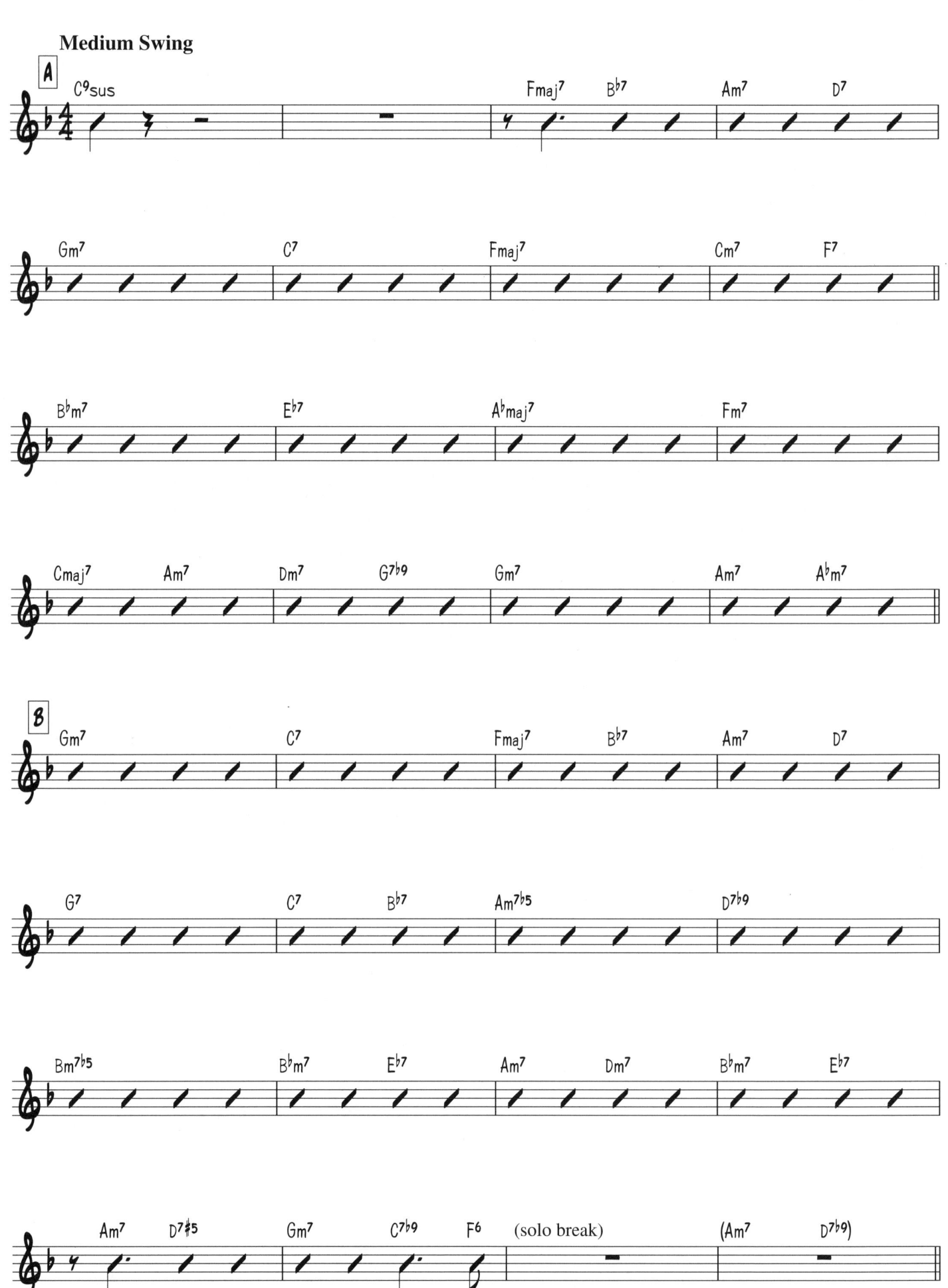

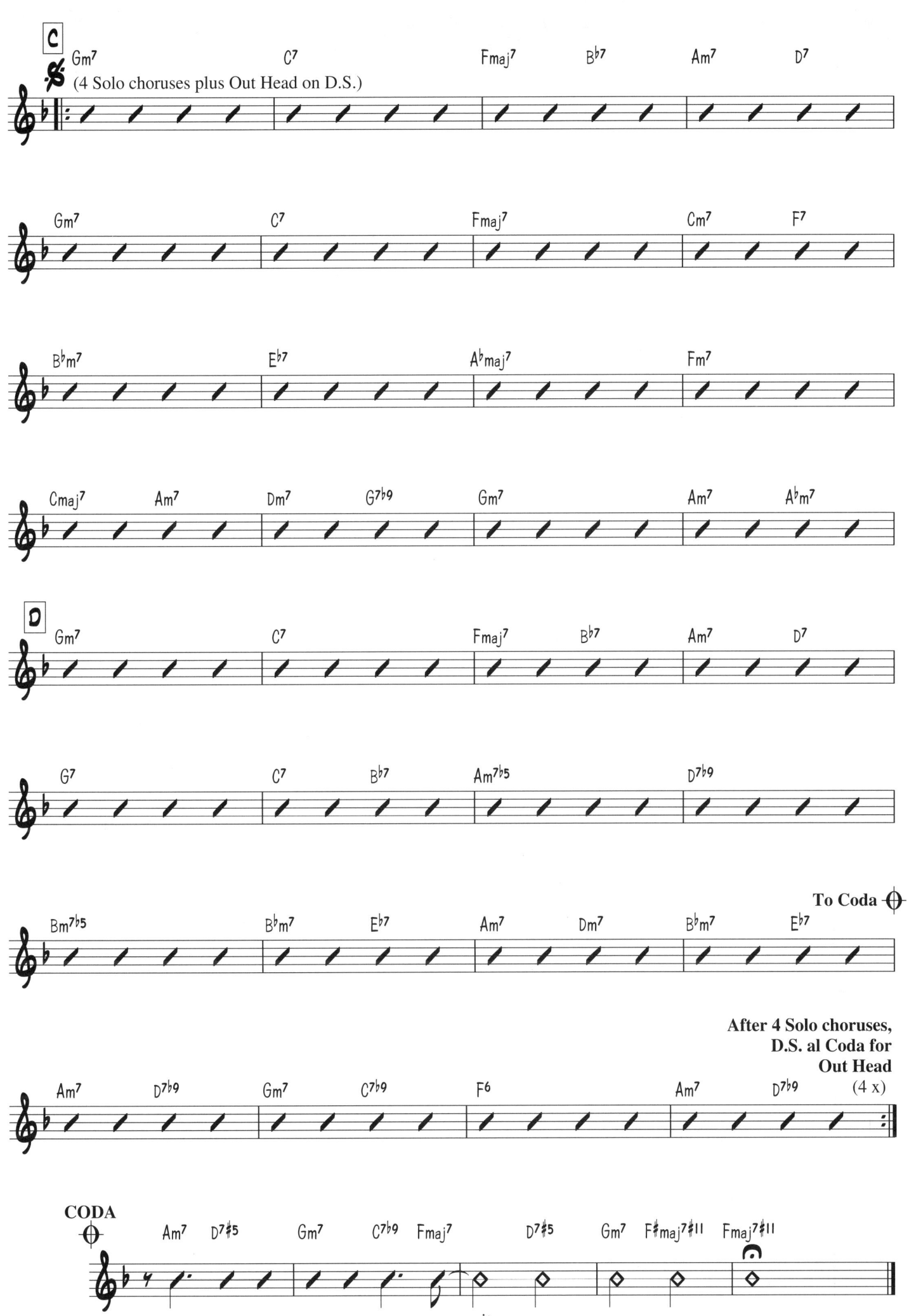

Just Friends

—John Klenner/Sam M. Lewis

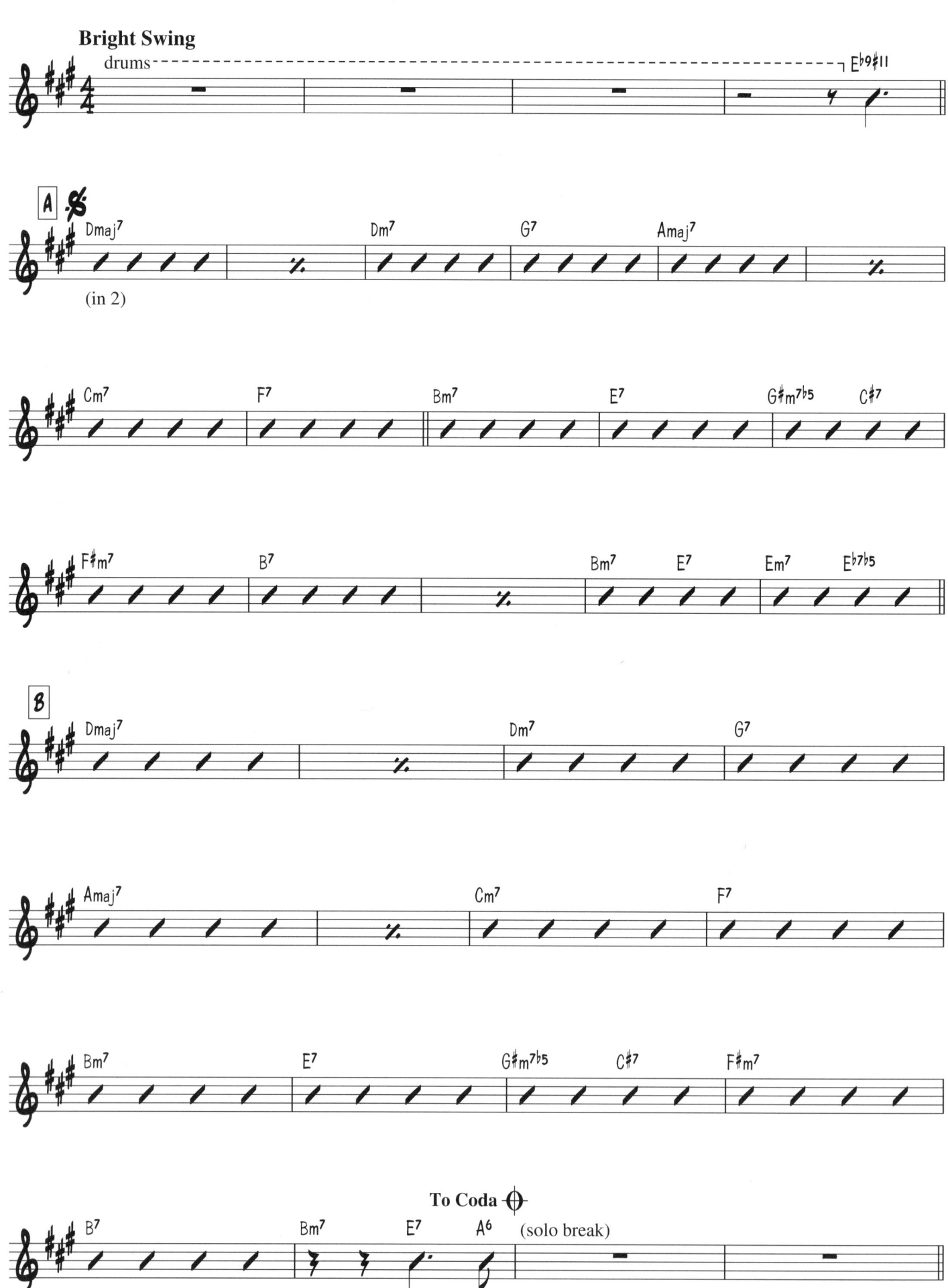

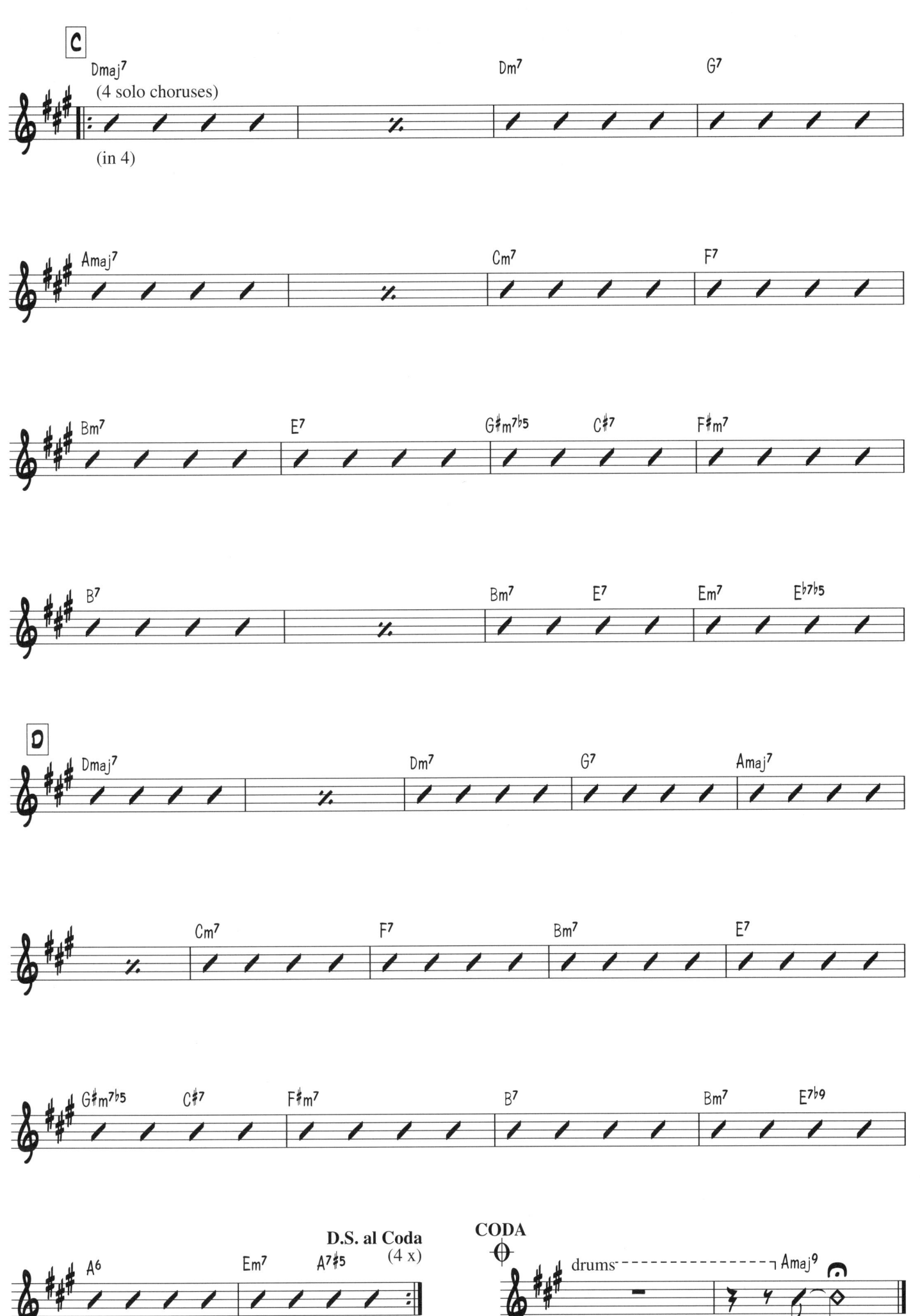

Like Someone in Love

—Jimmy Van Heusen/Johnny Burke

Medium Swing

A

| Fmaj7 | E°7 | Dm7 | /C | G7/B | B♭°7 | Am7 | D7♭9 |

(6 choruses)

| Gm7 | | C7 | | Fmaj7 | | Cm7 | F7 |

| B♭maj7 | | Em7 | A7 | Dmaj7 | | | |

| Dm7 | | G7 | | Gm7 | | C7♯5 | |

B

| Fmaj7 | E°7 | Dm7 | /C | G7/B | B♭°7 | Am7 | D7♭9 |

| Gm7 | | C7 | | Fmaj7 | | Cm7 | F7 |

| B♭maj7 | | Em7 | A7 | Dmaj7 | | G♯°7 | |

1.–5.

| Am7 | D7 | Gm7 | C7 | F6 | | Gm7 | C7 |

6.

| Am7 | D7♭9 | Gm7 | C7♭9 | C♯maj7 Dmaj7 Emaj7 F♯maj7 | Fmaj7 Emaj7 F6/9 |

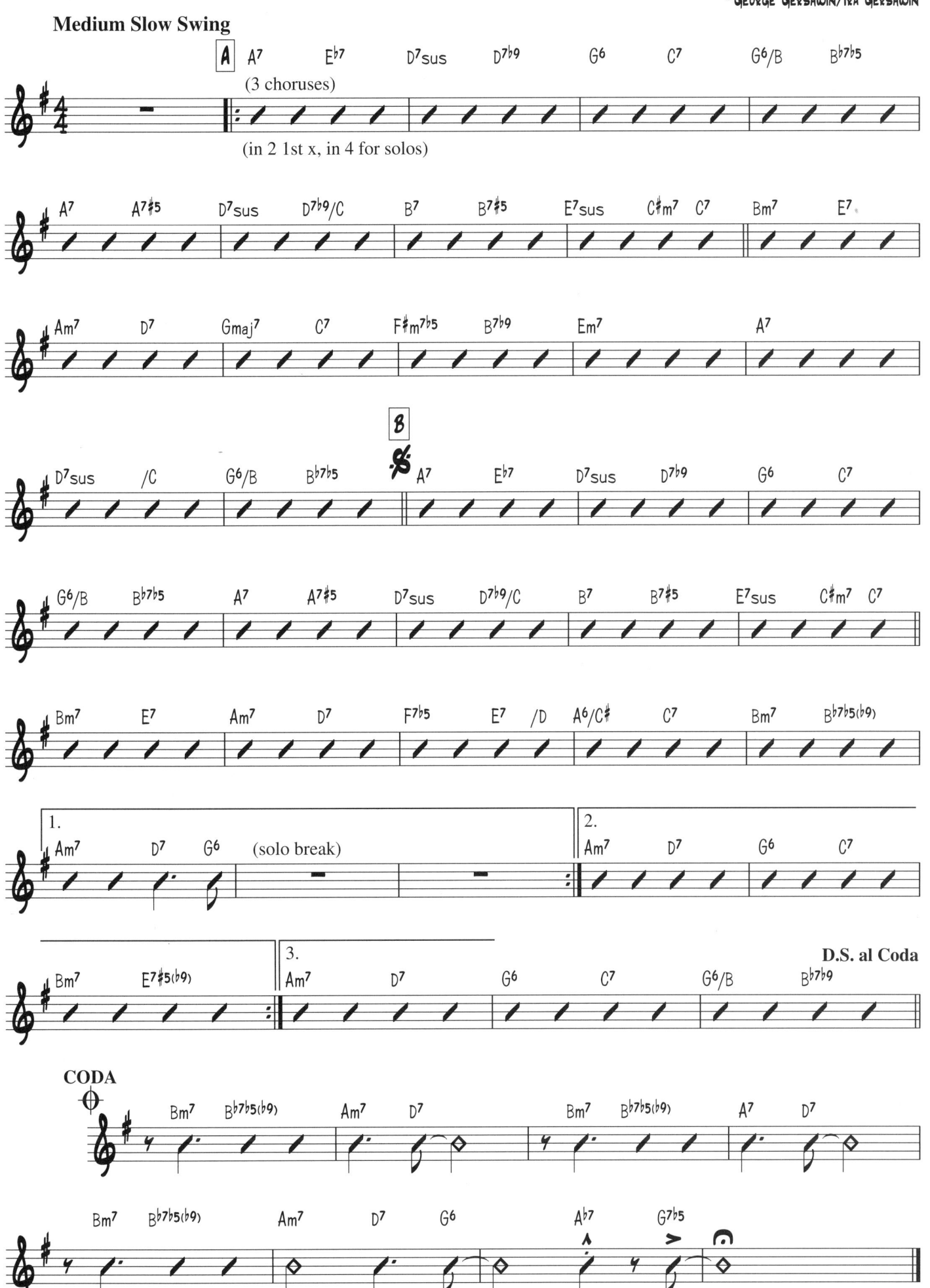

Maiden Voyage

—Herbie Hancock

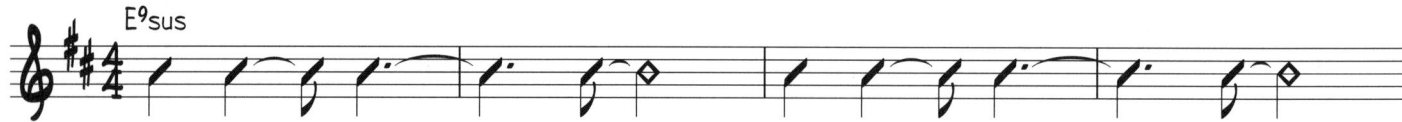
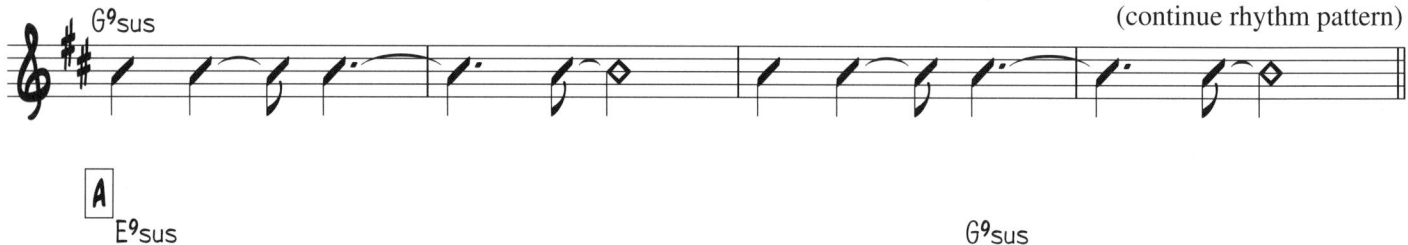

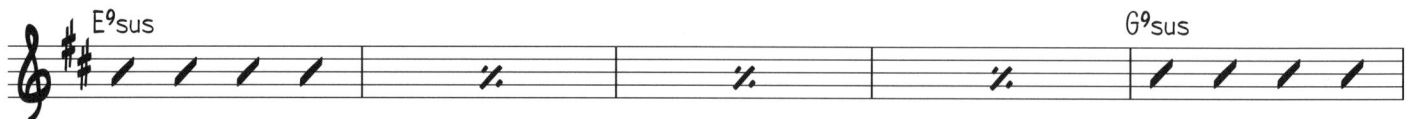
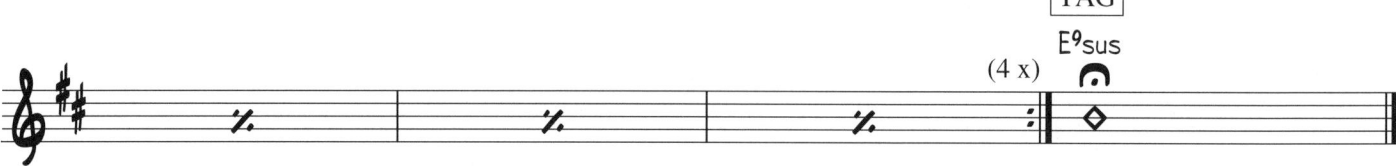

Mr. P.C.

—John Coltrane

Misty

My Funny Valentine

–Richard Rodgers/Lorenz Hart

Ballad – Double x Samba Feel on D.C.

A | Dm | Dm(maj7) | Dm7 | Dm6 |

1. | Bbmaj7 | Gm7 | Em7b5 | A7#5(b9) |

2. | Bbmaj7 Am7 | Gm7 | Gm7b5 | C7sus C7b9 |

B | Fmaj7 Gm7 | % | % | % |
C pedal ----------------------------------

| Fmaj7 | E7#5(b9) A7b9 Dm7 C#7 | Cm7 F7b9 Bbmaj7 | Em7b5 A7b9 |

C | Dm | Dm(maj7) | Dm7 | Dm6 | Bbmaj7 |

To Coda ⊕

| Em7b5 A7b9 | Dm7 G7#5(#9) | Cm7 B9 Bbmaj7 | Am7 Ab9 Gm7 C7b9 |

D.C. al Coda   **CODA**

| Fmaj9/C C9sus | Fmaj9/C Em7b5 A7b9 | ⊕ Bbmaj7 Am7 Ab9 | Gm7 C7b9 |
rit.

A Little Slower (Ballad Feel)

| Fmaj7 Gm7 | % | Fmaj7 Gm7 | % | Fmaj7 |
C pedal ----------------------------------

Nica's Dream

—Horace Silver

Night and Day

—Cole Porter

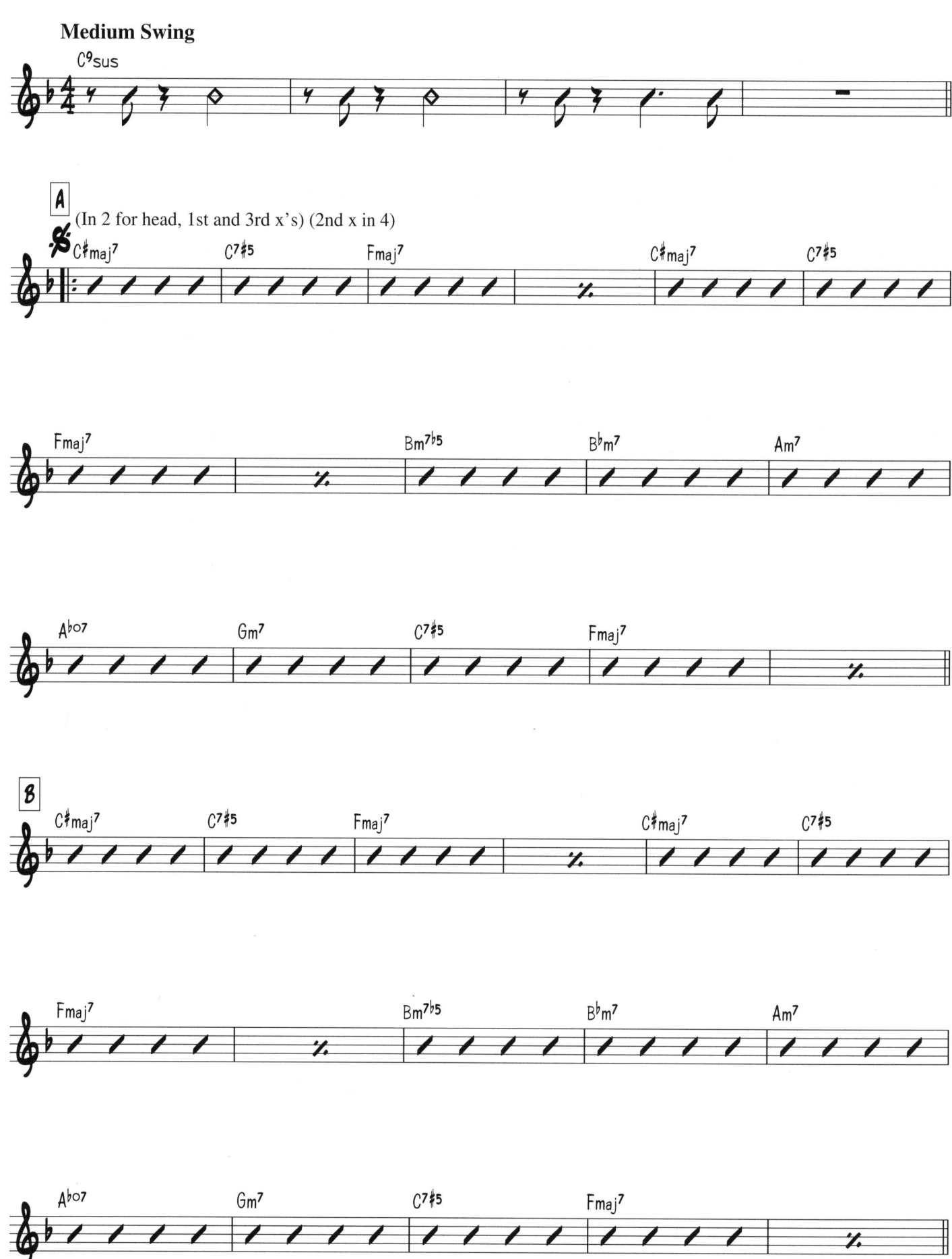

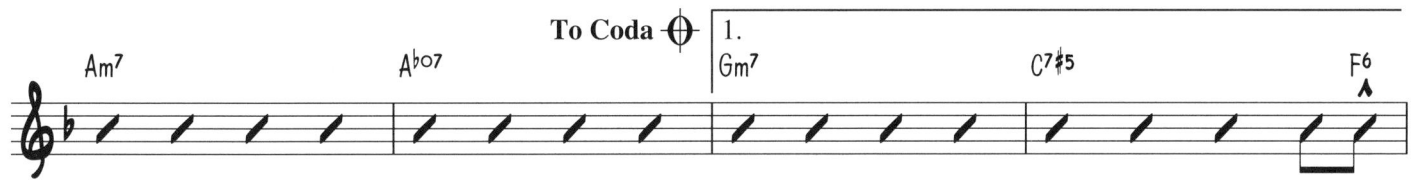
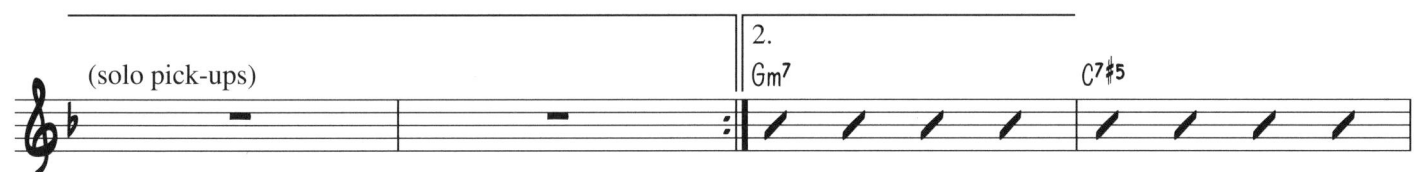
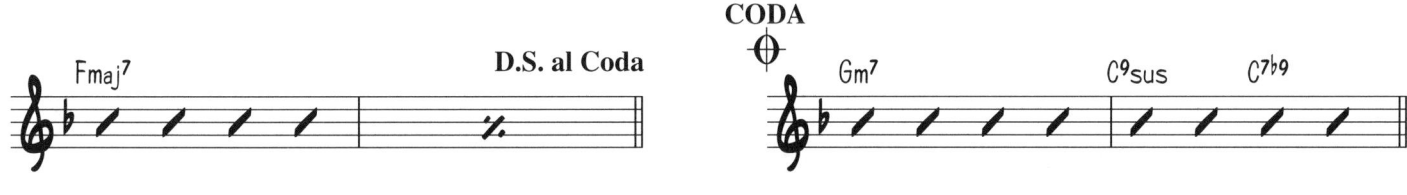
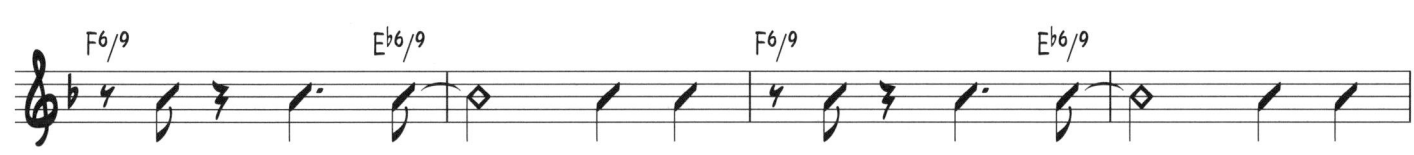
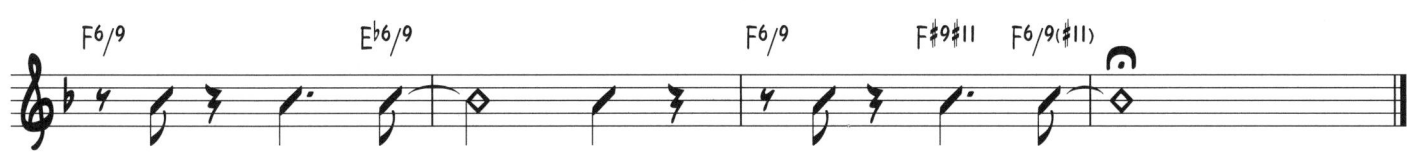

A Night in Tunisia

—Joseph Kosma/Johnny Mercer/Jacques Prevert

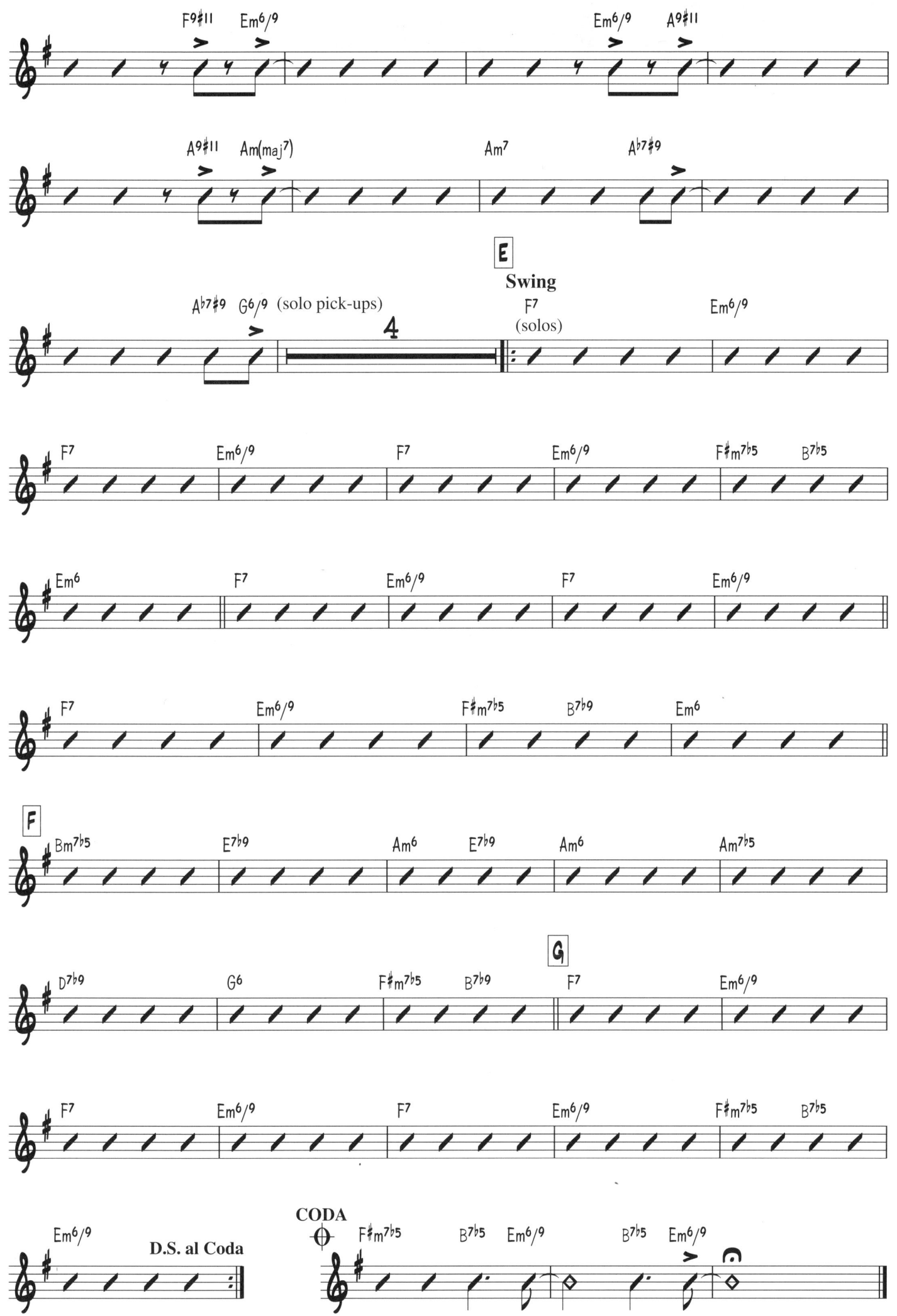

On Green Dolphin Street

—Bronislau Kaper/Ned Washington

Medium Latin

[A] (4 choruses) Latin

| D6/9 | | Fmaj7/D | |

| Emaj7/D | Ebmaj7/D | D6/9 | F#m7 B7b9 |

[B] **Swing**

| Em7 | A9sus A7b9 | D6/9 | Am7 D7b9 |

| Gm7 | C9sus C7b9 | Fmaj7 | Em7 A7b9 |

[C] **Latin**

| D6/9 | (simile) | Fmaj7/D | (simile) |

| Emaj7/D | Ebmaj7/D | D6/9 | F#m7b5 B7b9 |

[D] **Swing**

| Em7   /D | C#m7b5 F#7b9 | Bm7 | G#m7b5 C#7b9 |

| F#m7 B7b9 | Em7 A7b9 | 1.–3. Dmaj7   Em7 A7b9 :|| 4. Dmaj7 𝄐 ||

This piece is often performed in the key of E♭.

One Note Samba
(Samba de uma nota só)

—Antonio Carlos Jobim/Newton Mendonça

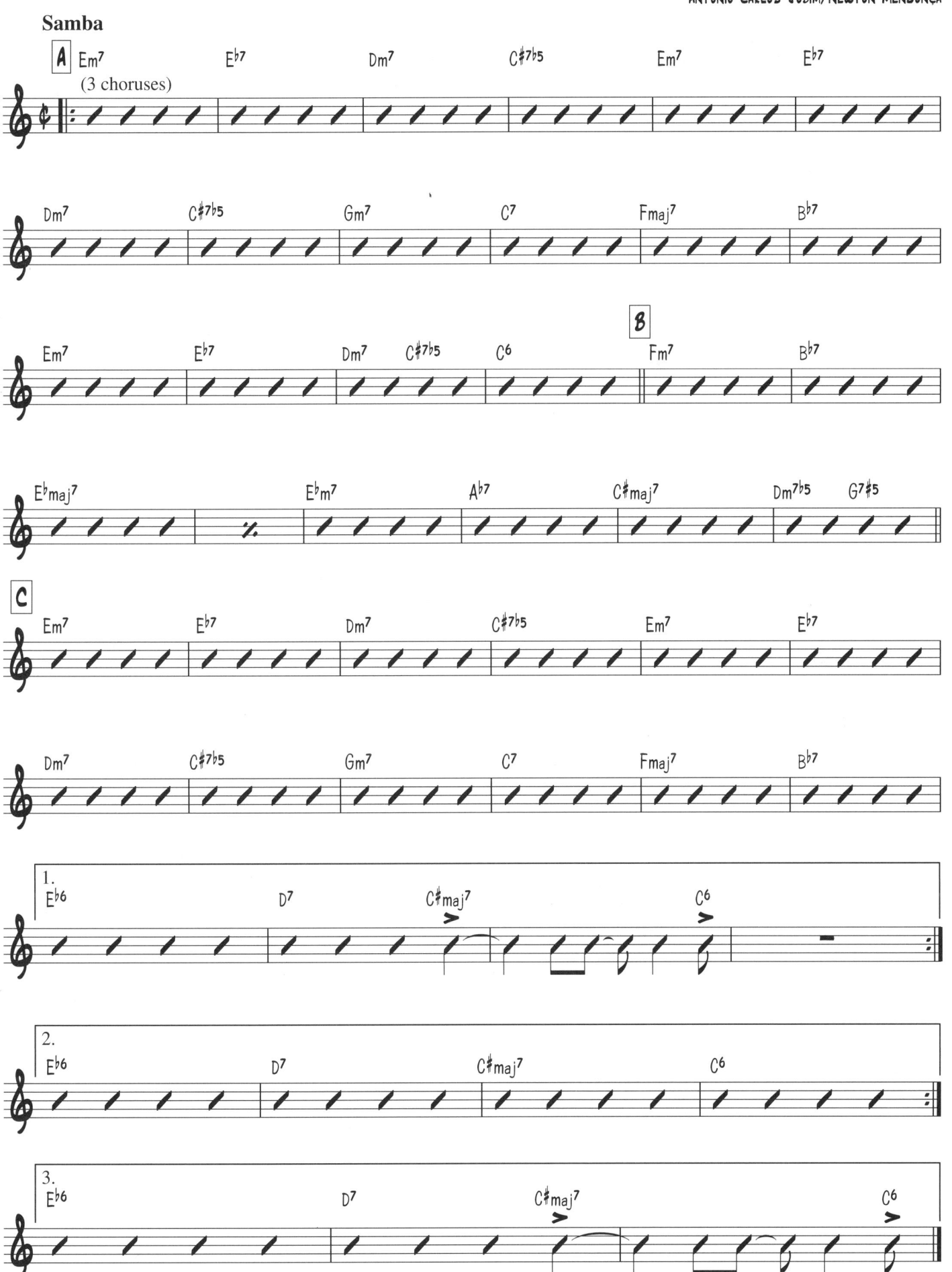

Perdido

—Juan Tizol/H.J. Lengsfelder/Ervin Drake

So What

—Miles Davis

Secret Love

—Sammy Fain/Paul Francis Webster

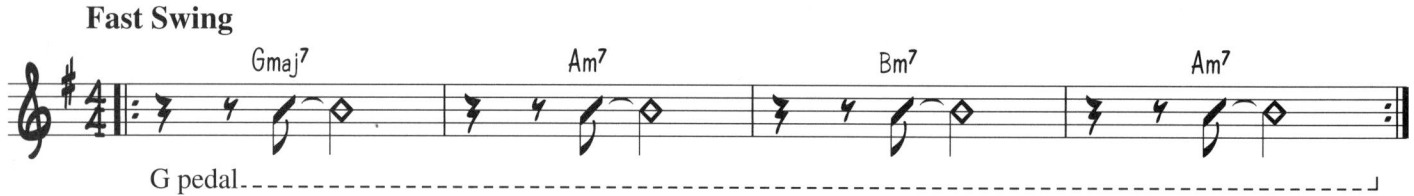

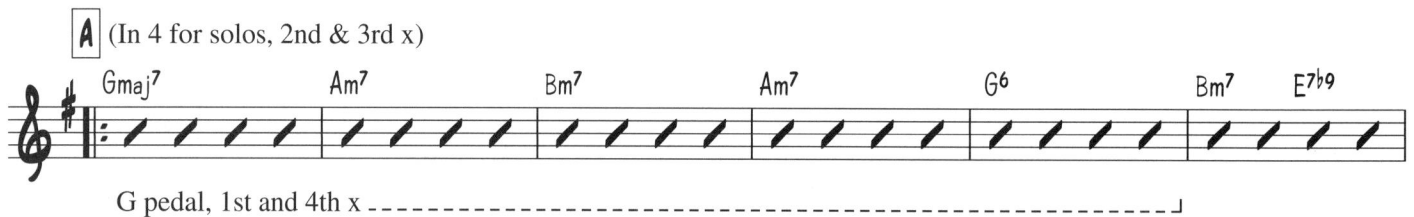

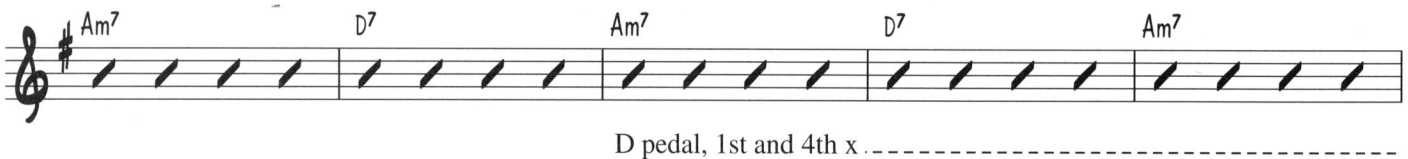

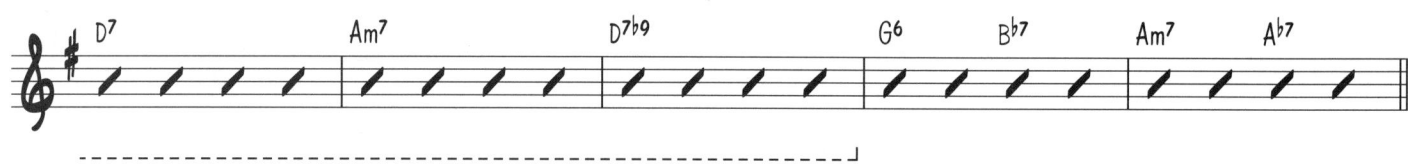

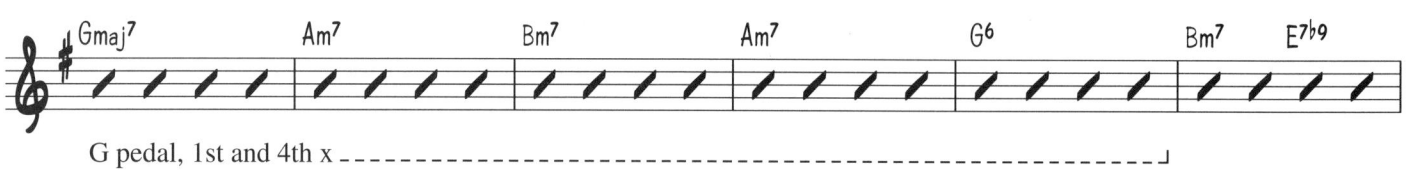

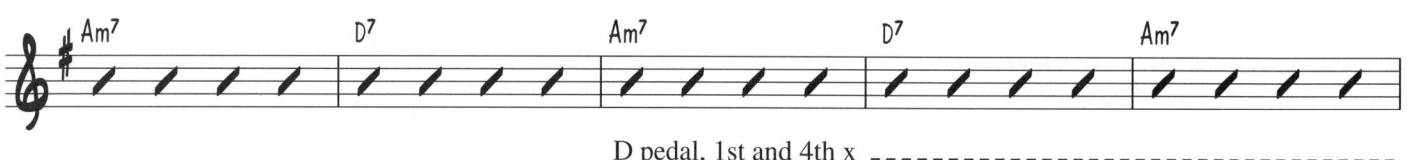

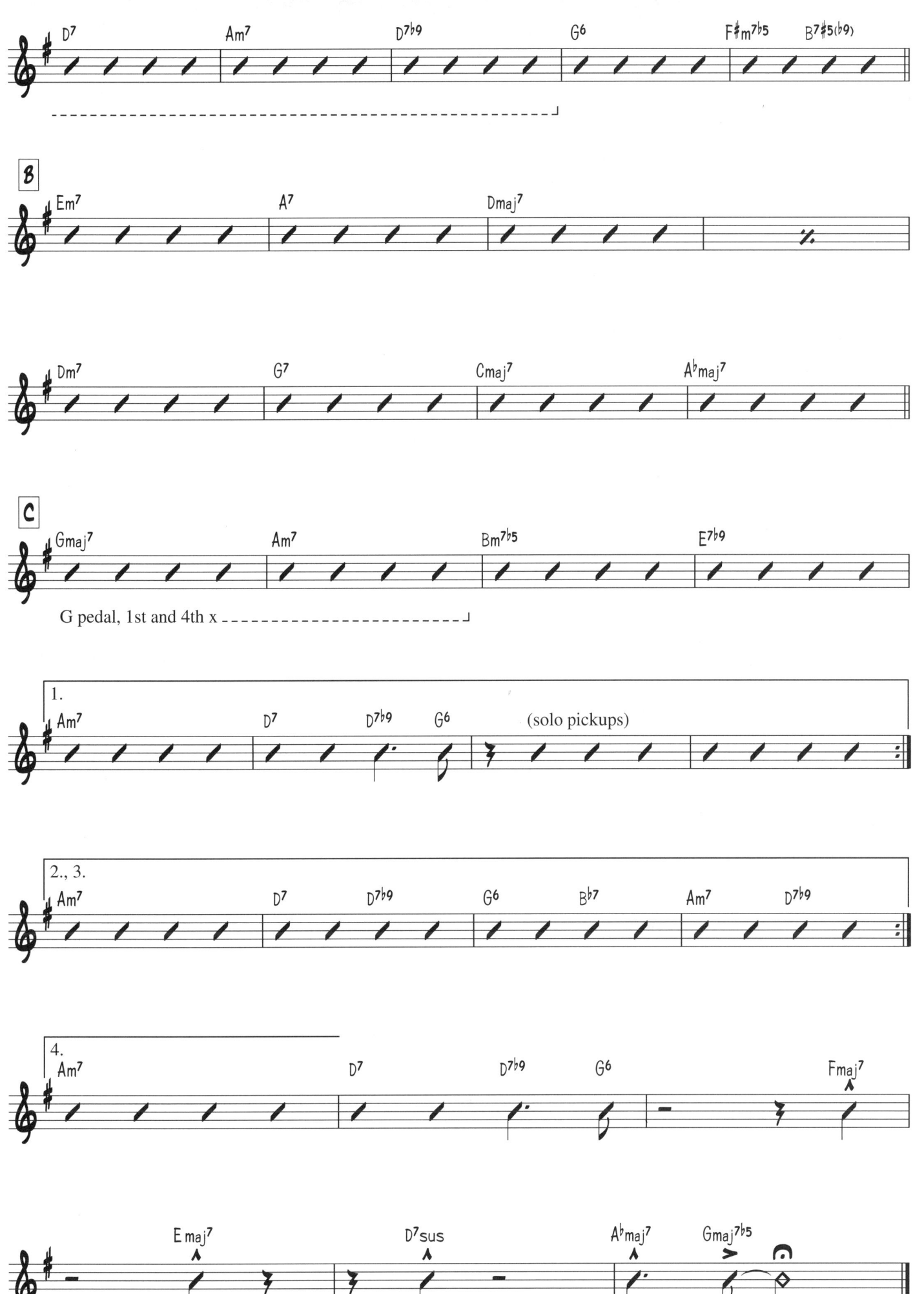

Softly As in a Morning Sunrise

Star Eyes

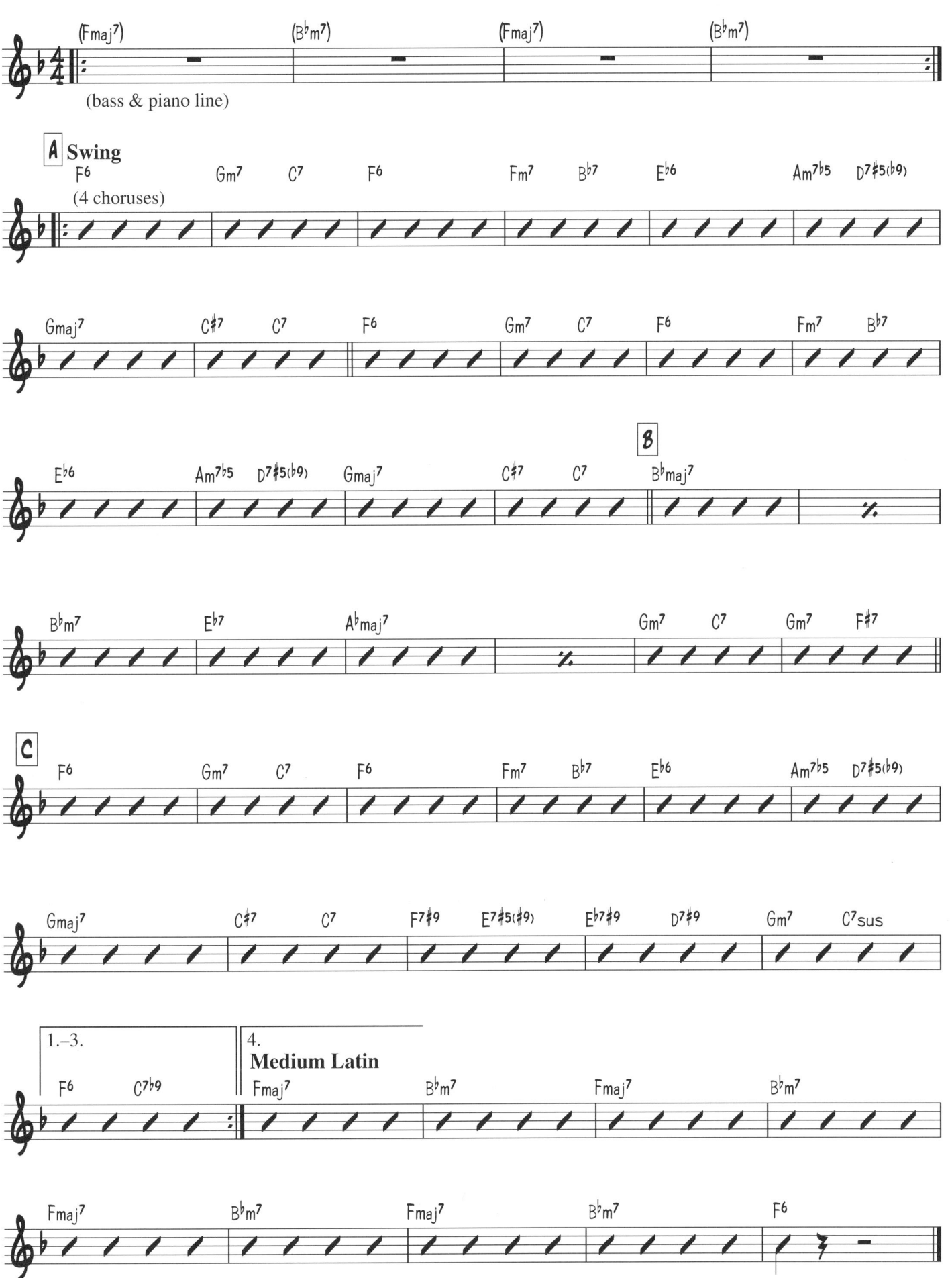

Speak Low

Stella by Starlight

—Victor Young/Ned Washingtoon

Ballad

A
F#m7b5	B7b9	Dm7	G7
Gm7	C7	Fmaj7	Bb7
Cmaj7	F#m7b5 B7b9	Em7	Cm7 F7
Gmaj7	F#m7b5 B7b9	Bm7b5	E7b9

B
| A7#5 | Dm7 (%) | Dm7 | (%) |
| Bb9#11 | Cmaj7 (%) | Cmaj7 | (%) |

C
| F#m7b5 | B7b9 | Em7b5 | A7b9 |
| Dm7b5 | G7b9 | 1. Cmaj7 | (%) :|

2.
| Cmaj7 | F7 | Cmaj7 | |

rit.

Take the "A" Train

—Billy Strayhorn

Tangerine

Things Ain't What They Used to Be

—Mercer Ellington

Wave

—Antonio Carlos Jobim

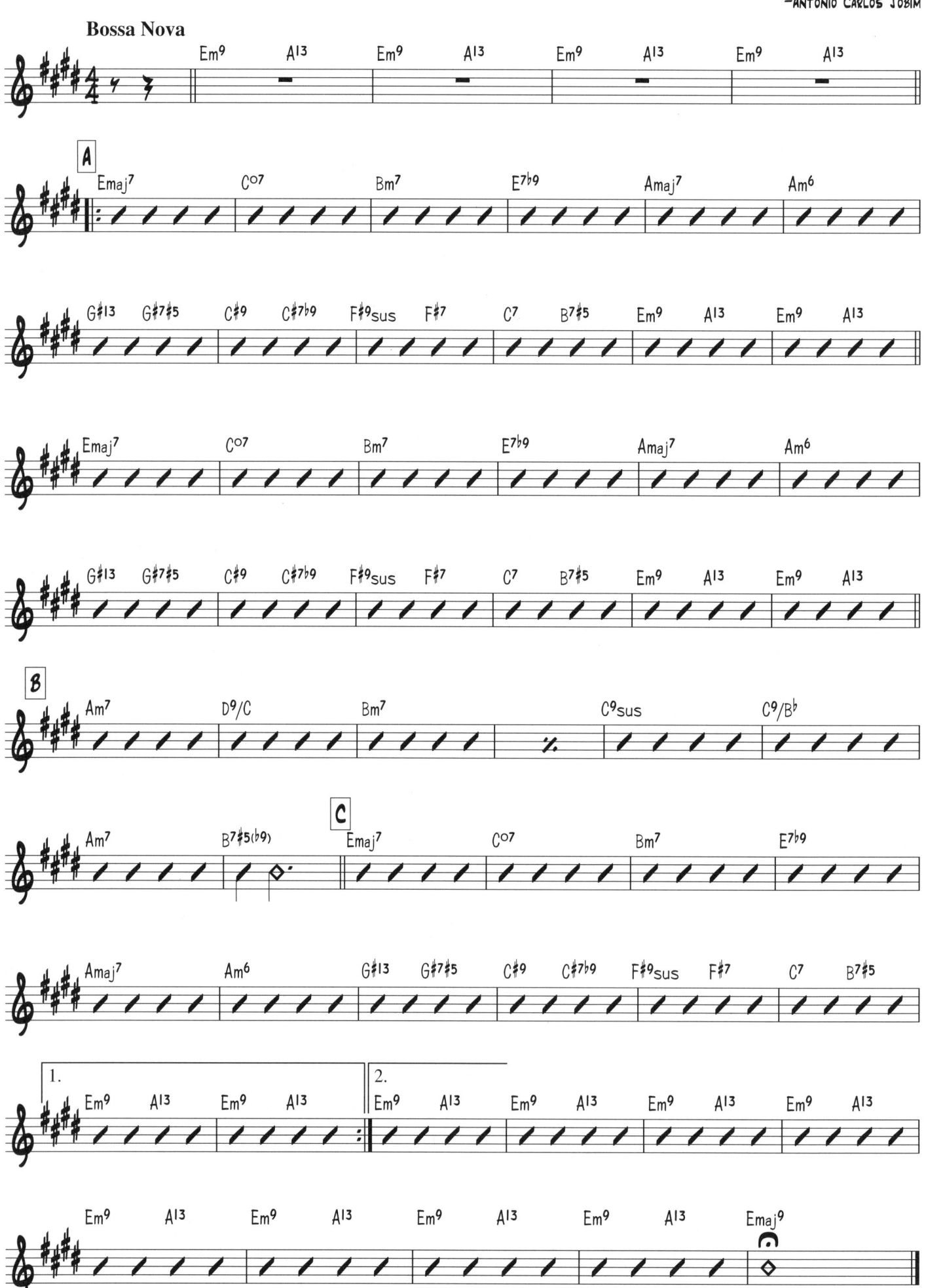

Yardbird Suite

—Charlie Parker

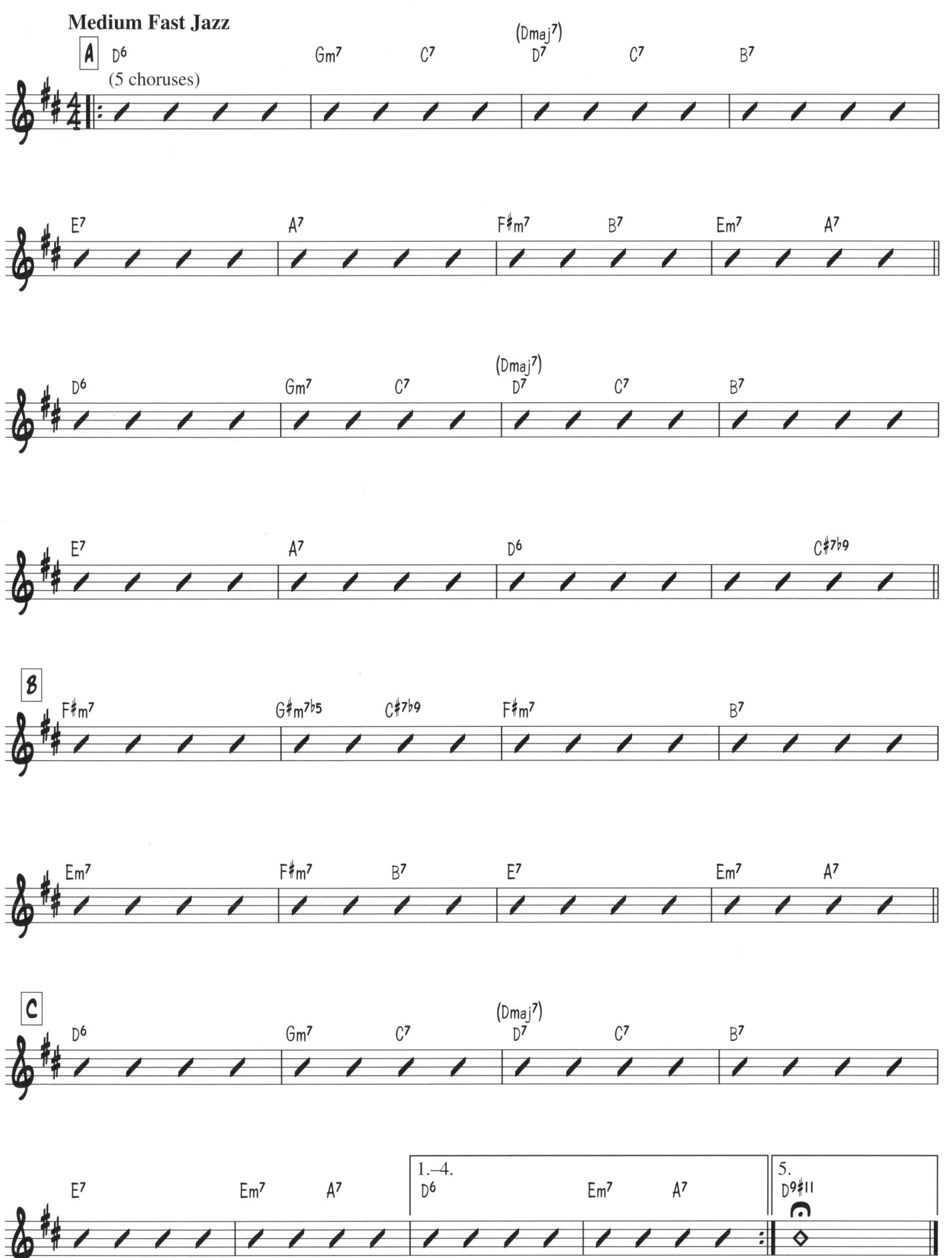

The Best-Selling Jazz Book of All Time Is Now Legal!

The Real Books are the most popular jazz books of all time. Since the 1970s, musicians have trusted these volumes to get them through every gig, night after night. The problem is that the books were illegally produced and distributed, without any regard to copyright law, or royalties paid to the composers who created these musical masterpieces.

Hal Leonard is very proud to present the first legitimate and legal editions of these books ever produced. You won't even notice the difference, other than all the notorious errors being fixed: the covers and typeface look the same, the song lists are nearly identical, and the price for our edition is even cheaper than the originals!

Every conscientious musician will appreciate that these books are now produced accurately and ethically, benefitting the songwriters that we owe for some of the greatest tunes of all time!

VOLUME 1
00240221	C Edition	$39.99
00240224	B♭ Edition	$39.99
00240225	E♭ Edition	$39.99
00240226	Bass Clef Edition	$39.99
00240292	C Edition 6 x 9	$35.00
00240339	B♭ Edition 6 x 9	$35.00
00451087	C Edition on CD-ROM	$29.99
00240302	A-D CD Backing Tracks	$24.99
00240303	E-J CD Backing Tracks	$24.95
00240304	L-R CD Backing Tracks	$24.95
00240305	S-Z CD Backing Tracks	$24.99
00110604	Book/USB Flash Drive Backing Tracks Pack	$79.99
00110599	USB Flash Drive Only	$50.00

VOLUME 2
00240222	C Edition	$39.99
00240227	B♭ Edition	$39.99
00240228	E♭ Edition	$39.99
00240229	Bass Clef Edition	$39.99
00240293	C Edition 6 x 9	$35.00
00125900	B♭ Edition 6 x 9	$35.00
00451088	C Edition on CD-ROM	$30.99
00240351	A-D CD Backing Tracks	$24.99
00240352	E-I CD Backing Tracks	$24.99
00240353	J-R CD Backing Tracks	$24.99
00240354	S-Z CD Backing Tracks	$24.99

VOLUME 3
00240233	C Edition	$39.99
00240284	B♭ Edition	$39.99
00240285	E♭ Edition	$39.99
00240286	Bass Clef Edition	$39.99
00240338	C Edition 6 x 9	$35.00
00451089	C Edition on CD-ROM	$29.99

VOLUME 4
00240296	C Edition	$39.99
00103348	B♭ Edition	$39.99
00103349	E♭ Edition	$39.99
00103350	Bass Clef Edition	$39.99

VOLUME 5
00240349	C Edition	$35.00

Also available:
00240264	The Real Blues Book	$34.99
00310910	The Real Bluegrass Book	$29.99
00240440	The Trane Book	$22.99
00240137	Miles Davis Real Book	$19.95
00240355	The Real Dixieland Book C Edition	$29.99
00122335	The Real Dixieland Book B♭ Edition	$29.99
00240235	The Duke Ellington Real Book	$19.99
00240268	The Real Jazz Solos Book	$30.00
00240348	The Real Latin Book C Edition	$35.00
00127107	The Real Latin Book B♭ Edition	$35.00
00240358	The Charlie Parker Real Book	$19.99
00240331	The Bud Powell Real Book	$19.99
00240437	The Real R&B Book	$39.99
00240313	The Real Rock Book	$35.00
00240323	The Real Rock Book – Vol. 2	$35.00
00240359	The Real Tab Book	$32.50
00240317	The Real Worship Book	$29.99

THE REAL CHRISTMAS BOOK
00240306	C Edition	$29.99
00240345	B♭ Edition	$29.99
00240346	E♭ Edition	$29.99
00240347	Bass Clef Edition	$32.50
00240431	A-G CD Backing Tracks	$24.99
00240432	H-M CD Backing Tracks	$24.99
00240433	N-Y CD Backing Tracks	$24.99

THE REAL VOCAL BOOK
00240230	Volume 1 High Voice	$35.00
00240307	Volume 1 Low Voice	$35.00
00240231	Volume 2 High Voice	$35.00
00240308	Volume 2 Low Voice	$35.00
00240391	Volume 3 High Voice	$35.00
00240392	Volume 3 Low Voice	$35.00
00118318	Volume 4 High Voice	$35.00
00118319	Volume 4 Low Voice	$35.00

THE REAL BOOK – STAFF PAPER
00240327	$10.99

HOW TO PLAY FROM A REAL BOOK
For All Musicians
by Robert Rawlins
00312097	$17.50

Complete song lists online at www.halleonard.com
Prices, content, and availability subject to change without notice.

7777 W. BLUEMOUND RD. P.O. BOX 13819 MILWAUKEE, WI 53213